JACKSON HAINES

The Skating King

Ryan Stevens

Canadian Cataloguing in Publication Data

Title: Jackson Haines: The Skating King
Author: Stevens, Ryan, 1982-
ISBN: 9781738768219

Copyright © 2023
by Ryan Stevens

Independently published
All rights reserved

Every reasonable effort has been made to cite and/or credit all source material included in this book.

If errors or omissions have occurred, they will be corrected in future editions provided written notification and supporting documentation has been received by the author.

Ere skaters' art emerged from haze
There flashed across the dark — ablaze -
The star that showed the gleaming way
To where enchantment reigns.
From the Western World he came
In ancient cities finding fame,
Where beauty lovers felt the sway,
The lure of Jackson Haines.

Before their Kaisers, Czars and Kings
With subtle grace he glides and swings,
While dancing Austria joyed to see
The realm of treasure there.
The Russian loved a lighter mood,
So fancy dress his fancy wooed;
Superbly skating Haines might be
Dundreary or a bear.

He saw no more his native land;
He followed frost's bewitching hand
And if fate gave him ice and art,
He asked for nothing more.
There's but the waltz which bear his names
As epitaph to Jackson Haines;
For having keenly played his part,
He lies on Finland's shore.

A. Ralph Keighley
"Skating" magazine, January 1931

TABLE OF CONTENTS

Introduction	8
1838-1863	11
1864	35
1865	50
1866	57
1867	66
1868	73
1869	81
1870	86
1871	93
1872	104
1873	110
1874	115
1875	122
The Legacy	130
Family History	155

Competitions	168
Acknowledgements	171
Visual Material	175
Author's Note	181
Other Books	182

INTRODUCTION

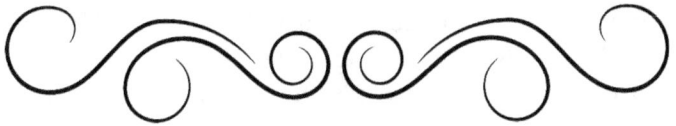

What is remembered about us when we are gone? Is it the truth or whatever makes the best story?

For well over a century, murky legends of figure skating's founding father Jackson Haines have been an integral part of the sport's oral and written history.

In the many years since his death, Jackson has been hailed as a skater, ballet master, Indian club juggler, truck driver and actor. Chroniclers of the sport, writing in sweeping artistic terms with great conviction, have weaved various narratives about him.

Here is what you have probably read about The Skating King over the years:

He was born in 1840. He was born in Chicago to Canadian parents. He was born in Troy. He was born in Canada. His father was rich. His wife's name was Anna. He won the Championships of America in 1863, 1864 and/or 1865. He wasn't popular in America. He wasn't popular in England. Vienna was the only place that accepted him. He died in 1879.

Not a single one of those statements is true. One of the main reasons these talking points have been repeated so many times over the years is that they originally came from widely read early 20th Century books that were otherwise quite reliable.

Through in-depth research in archives and nineteenth century primary sources, "Jackson Haines: The Skating King" aims to present an accurate account of the fascinating life of a man who forever changed the face of the world's most exciting sport.

It is time to separate the man from the myth and learn about the real Jackson Haines.

1838-1863

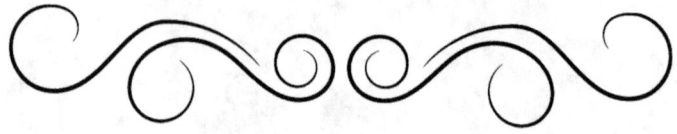

Jackson Harris[1] Haines was born in the autumn of 1838 in New York City.[2] He was the son of Elizabeth Terhune Earle and Alexander Frazee[3] Haines, a fruit dealer[4] who was affiliated with the Park & Tilford grocery store[5] and

---

1   "History and Genealogy of the Earles of Secaucus; With an Account of Other English and American Branches", Isaac Newton Earle, 1925; Pedigree Sheet (Haines and Earle genealogy) submitted by Mrs. Lois Shaffer, World Figure Skating Museum and Hall of Fame. Records obtained February 11, 1953.
2   "The Illustrated Sporting News", September 17, 1864; "Laibacher Zeitung", October 31, 1867; "Drammens Blad", January 16, 1872; "Åbo Underrättelser", November 19, 1872; "Hämäläinen", March 4, 1875. "The Illustrated Sporting News" gives Jackson's birth year as 1838. The "Laibacher Zeitung" from Ljubljana provides Jackson's date of birth as October 4, 1838, while the "Åbo Underrättelser" states that he was born on December 4, 1838. All of these newspaper articles note that he was born in New York, which agrees with Census records. An act requiring citizens to register births, marriages and deaths in the State of New York was not instituted until 1847.
3   New York DAR GRC Report; S2 V029: Unpublished Bible and Family Records Together With Genealogical Notes and Other Authentic Data
4   United States Census, 1860
5   "The Father of Figure Skating", Winfield A. Hird, "Skating"

a wholesale fruit shop at Pierce's Italian Warehouse on Broadway.[6]

Jackson was of British, Dutch and Hungarian ancestry. Through his paternal line, he was a descendant of Owain the Great - the King of Gwynedd, North Wales[7] who led a war against King Henry II in the eleventh century and Deacon Samuel Haines, a Puritan settler of New England in the seventeenth century.[8] His maternal grandmother's family, the Westervelts, were early Dutch settlers of Long Island.[9] On his maternal grandfather's side, he was a direct descendant of Edward Earle[10], a wealthy slave plantation owner and Justice of the Peace who bought Secaucus Island in 1676[11] and Morris Earle

---

magazine, January 1941; "Dressing Room Chatter", Jack Minnoch, "Evening Recorder" (Amsterdam, NY), January 24, 1941

6 Advertisements, "New York Daily Herald", October 29, 1853; Trow's City Directory, 1856 and 1857 editions; Advertisements, "The New York Times", March 12, 1861

7 "Owen of Wales: The End of the House of Gwynedd", Anthony D. Carr, 1991

8 "Deacon Samuel Haines of Westbury, Wiltshire, England and His Descendants in America 1635-1901", Thomas Vanburen Haines, Andrew Mack Haines, 1902

9 "The Father of Figure Skating", Winfield A. Hird, "Skating" magazine, January 1941; "Dressing Room Chatter", Jack Minnoch, "Evening Recorder" (Amsterdam, NY), January 24, 1941

10 "History and Genealogy of the Earles of Secaucus; With an Account of Other English and American Branches", Isaac Newton Earle, 1925

11 "History of Secaucus, New Jersey in Commemoration of the Fiftieth Anniversary of Its Independence: Emphasizing Its

Sr. of Hackensack, New Jersey, a soldier in the American Revolutionary War.[12]

Jackson's paternal grandfather,[13] whom he was named after, operated the Haines & Hunter grocery firm on the corner of Partition and Washington Streets and served as an assessor for New York City's Third Ward.[14]

One of five children, Jackson had an older brother and sister, Eugene and Sarah Augusta and two younger sisters, Hannah Maria and Elizabeth.[15]

Jackson grew up in the part of New York City now known as the West Village[16]. His family lived in a series of homes near Washington Square, on what is now the west side of Seventh Avenue. The Haines family moved at least five times in the same area during Jackson's

---

    Earlier Development, 1900-1950", Gertrude Scholl Reed, Robert Edward Henkel, 1950; "Meet The Tredwells: The Ancestry of Eliza Tredwell, Part 1", Ann Haddad, Merchants House Museum blog, March 28, 2019

12 "Lineage Book, Vol. 77", Daughters of the American Revolution, 1925

13 New York, New York, U.S., Extracted Death Index, 1862-1948

14 "Longworth's American Almanac, New-York Register, and City Directory, for the Thirty- Eighth Year of American Independence", 1813; "Third Ward", "New York Evening Post", July 11, 1820; "Died", "New York Evening Post", April 9, 1821

15 New York State Census, 1855; United States Census, 1860

16 Correspondence with Greg Young, The Bowery Boys Podcast, April 2, 2013; "The Village's lovely Rhinelander Row", Esther Crain, "Ephemeral New York", April 7, 2009

youth - renting rooms on Cornelia, Minnetta, Bleecker, Fourth and Bethune Streets.[17]

Though his family was not wealthy, they had connections through his grandfather's position with the City. They also had ties to Abraham Stagg, a Grand Sachem at Tammany Hall, whose daughter was married to a relative of Jackson's mother's.[18]

From a young age, Jackson was exposed to the arts. He was tutored in music, dance and French and attended a wide variety of theatrical productions with his family.[19] Living shoulder to shoulder with boarders, like a musician from Russia and a bookseller from Holland[20], gave him an appreciation for cultural diversity.

In Jackson's youth, one of New York City's most popular skating spots was the old Beekman Pond, which at the time extended beyond Madison Avenue from Fifty-Ninth Street and Sixth Avenue. The ice was divided

---

17 Trow's City Directory, 1846-1864 editions; 1840 United States Census; 1850 United States Census; 1855 New York State Census; 1860 United States Census

18 Land Grants from Abraham Stagg to Hannah and Alex F. Haines, May 14, 1834; "Cases in the Court of Appeals of the State of New-York", 1855; "History and Genealogy of the Earles of Secaucus; With an Account of Other English and American Branches", Isaac Newton Earle, 1925

19 "The Father of Figure Skating", Winfield A. Hird, "Skating" magazine, January 1941; "Dressing Room Chatter", Jack Minnoch, "Evening Recorder" (Amsterdam, NY), January 24, 1941

20 United States Census, 1860

into three private skating areas[21], frequented by thousands of enthusiastic skaters of all abilities and classes during the long winters.[22] An 1880 article in "Truth" recalled, "The Beekman Pond was cut up by the filling in of Fifth and Madison avenues, and Hugh Mitchell took the south-east corner of Fifth Avenue and Fifty-Ninth street, happy old Major Oatman the south-east corner and Alex. MacMillan, afterward, the south-east corner of Madison Avenue and Fifty-Ninth street, for private ponds, which flourished for years, but are now entirely filled up and otherwise occupied."[23]

In the 1850s, Fifty-Ninth Street was viewed as an invisible line dividing 'the classes and the masses'. Below the Street lived the well-to-do, with their fancy hats and fashionable businesses, among them a Pearl Street vendor named Frederick Stevens who sold "skates and straps of every description [with] Fogg's patent lever buckle on straps."[24] Above Fifty-Ninth Street, through a waste land later incorporated into Central Park, were thousands of poor souls living in deplorable conditions in 'Squatter's Sovereignty', many as a result of The Panic of 1857[25]. Public health pioneer Hermann Michael Biggs recalled, "The squatters' settlements in the Park were

---

21 "Skating and the Skaters", "Truth", December 10, 1880
22 "At The Central Park", "The New York Times", January 3, 1862
23 "Skating and the Skaters", "Truth", December 10, 1880
24 Advertisement, "The New York Times", January 10, 1862
25 "Déjà Vu All Over Again: Agency, Uncertainty, Leverage and the Panic of 1857", Timothy J. Riddiough, Howard E. Thompson, "HKIMR Working Paper"

surrounded by swamps, and overgrown with briers, vines and thickets. The soil that covered the rocky surface was unfit for cultivation. Here and there were stone quarries and stagnant ponds. In this wilderness lived the squatters, in little shanties and huts made of boards picked up along the river fronts and often pieced out with sheets of tin, obtained by flattening cans. Some occupants paid $10 to $25 rent, but the majority paid nothing... Some of the shanties were dugouts and most had dirt floors. In this manner lived, in a state of loose morality, Americans, Germans, Irish, Negroes and Indians. Some were honest and some were not; many were roughs and crooks. Much of their food was refuse, which they procured in the lower portion of the City, and carried along Fifth Avenue to their homes in small carts drawn by dogs. The mongrel dogs were a remarkable feature of squatter life, and it is said that the Park area contained no less than one hundred thousand 'curs of low degree', which, with cows, pigs, cats, goats, geese and chickens, roamed at will, and lived upon the refuse, which was everywhere."[26]

On the corner of Fifth Avenue and Thirty-Ninth Street was W.H. Disbrow's Riding Academy. William Henry Disbrow was an enterprising business owner who was willing to try just about anything to draw in patrons. He sold horses, carriages, wagons, harnesses and saddles[27] and offered riding lessons to both men and women. He also operated a pond and Skating Gymnasium on his

---

26 "Preventive Medicine in the City of New York", Volume 9, Hermann Michael Biggs, 1897
27 Advertisement, "New York Daily Herald", May 31, 1861

grounds, offering "instruction and exercise" on both ice and roller skates.[28] In those days, ice skating was known as 'fancy' skating and roller skates were referred to as 'parlour' or 'saloon' skates.

Richard Westervelt Earle gave his nephew 'Jack' his first pair of ice skates, and he learned the basics of skating on the frozen gutters and streets of New York.[29] By the age of twelve, Jackson was already quite adept at the art of skating, devoting much of his free time to practicing at Disbrow's Skating Academy[30], the old Beekman Pond[31], a stone's throw from 'Squatter's Sovereignty' and the Central Park Skating Pond[32] with his sister Elizabeth[33].

'Jersey John' Engler, a tinsmith who was one of New York City's best-known skaters during that era, claimed to have taught him "how to cut all sorts of fancy

---

28 Advertisement, "The New York Times", January 10, 1862
29 Interview with Vivian Vreeland Mausler, great-granddaughter of Richard Westervelt Earle. "Descendants of Morris Earle and Elizabeth Terhune Through the Fourth Generation", Joseph W. Dooley, March 6, 2023
30 Correspondence with the National Skating Association, George Henry Browne, 1891 and 1901, cited in "Ice Abroad: From The British Archives", Dennis L. Bird, "Skating" magazine, February 1978
31 "Skating and the Skaters", "Truth", December 10, 1880
32 "Jackson Haines, The Champion Skater Of The World", "The Illustrated Sporting News", September 17, 1864
33 "The Father of Figure Skating", Winfield A. Hird, "Skating" magazine, January 1941; "Dressing Room Chatter", Jack Minnoch, "Evening Recorder" (Amsterdam, NY), January 24, 1941

figures".³⁴

Jackson soon came up with the idea of translating ice skating to the stage.³⁵ To achieve his goal, he drew inspiration from the world of dance. New York City was home to over a dozen dance schools when he was a teenager. Among these were Brooke's Dancing Academy and Hillgrove's Dancing Academy, both located between Broadway and the Bowery, Mademoiselle Caroline Vezien's Dancing Academy on Howard Street and Madame C. Dubreul Ferrero and E. Ferrero's New York Dancing Academy at Montague Hall on Court Street in Brooklyn.³⁶ Schools of this nature offered instruction for men and women of all ages, teaching everything from polkas, waltzes and quadrilles to cotillions, boleros and the Highland fling.³⁷ At Dodsworth's Dancing Academy in Brooklyn, New Yorkers could even learn "the peculiar dances of Poland and Hungary, so popular at the present time in Vienna".³⁸

It is unknown which, if any, of these schools Jackson attended. We do know that he studied under an unnamed ballet master at one point.³⁹ A possible

---

34 "Veterans of the Ice: Engler, Father of Figure Skating", Bat Wright, "The Troy Times", January 9, 1919
35 "Der Schlittschuhläufer Haines", "Tagespost", August 17, 1867
36 "Dancing Academies", "New York Daily Herald", September 29, 1855
37 "The Brooklyn Daily Eagle", January 4, 1850
38 Advertisements, "New York Tribune", October 27, 1858
39 "Der Schlittschuhläufer Haines", "Tagespost", August 17, 1867

candidate was Frederick Dennstaedt, who was first hired as a ballet master by the New York Academy of Music in 1858. Frederick had studied in Berlin and performed at the Covent Garden Theatre in London before immigrating to America. He was also employed as a ballet master at the Winter Garden Theatre, where Jackson later performed.[40] Jackson also had exposure to ballet when he later toured with Annetta Galletti and Edouard Velarde, European ballet dancers who came to America with Italian choreographer Domenico Ronzani's troupe.[41]

In late August and early September of 1859, Wallack's Theater on Broadway presented a drama called "Geraldine" starring Irish-born actress Matilda Heron.[42] It was during the run of this show, on September 7, 1859, that Jackson gave his first public performance on parlour skates.[43] He had practiced for three months on level ground, overlooking the fact that the podium on

---

40 "New York Daily Herald", February 6, 1859; "New York Daily Herald", October 12, 1859; "New York Court of Appeals, Records and Briefs", 1872
41 Broadside, "Mr. E.F. Keach : third week of the continued success of the great and unrivalled pantomimists, Fox's Ravel Troupe! : first appearance of the celebrated Annetta Galletti!... August 4, 1862"; "Champagne Charlie and Pretty Jemima: Variety Theater in the Nineteenth Century", Gillian M. Rodger, 2010; "Ballet in America - The Emergence of an American Art", George Amberg, 2013
42 Advertisements, "New York Daily Tribune", September 9, 1859
43 "Laibacher Zeitung", October 31, 1867

the Wallack's Theater stage had a slope[44], and viewed his debut performance as a failure.[45]

That winter, Jackson became one of the first thirty-five members of the original New York Skating Club[46] that met on the ponds of the newly incorporated Central Park. A report in the "New York Evening Express" noted, "Among the more expert skaters was a young man about twenty years of age, whose name our reporter ascertained to be Jackson Haines, and a grandson of Mr. Earle, the most celebrated skater of his day in the United States. He is a member of the New York Skating Club - which he has just joined - and is a most splendid and graceful skater - in fact, a perfect acrobat on skates... Mr. Haines was dressed in a blue flannel suit, with leather belt, similar to that worn by a base ball player, which was very appropriate."[47] Within two years, half a dozen other skating clubs had been formed in New York, among them the Washington Skating Club, the Nassau Skating Club for Ladies and Gentlemen, the Union Skating Association of Brooklyn, the Pastime Skating Club and the People's Independent Skating Club.[48] When The Red Ball was up, skating ponds were crowded and there were often disagreements

---

44 "Der Schlittschuhläufer Haines", "Tagespost", August 17, 1867
45 "Tages-Post", December 31, 1871
46 "Figures", "The New Yorker", January 29, 1927
47 "Central Park Skating", "New York Evening Express", December 28, 1859
48 "Ladies' Skating Costume", "The Brooklyn Daily Eagle", December 26, 1861

between figure skaters and those who indulged in the latest fad – baseball on ice.[49]

During the skating boom in New York, Jackson married Almira 'Alma' Bogart, a young woman from Manhattan who came from a somewhat scandalous background. In 1856, her father, a police justice[50] attached to The Tombs Police Court[51], was tried and convicted on the charge of malfeasance for "corruptly and maliciously accepting straw bail in the case of a pick-pocket".[52] Just two months after the New York Supreme Court made a ruling that he was liable to either a fine or imprisonment[53], he died at his home. He was remembered as a "large-hearted man... well-liked by all who knew him. His faults and misfortunes, whatever they were, arose from an impulse too generous and a confidence too implicit."[54] After Almira's father's death, her mother Mary Ann was forced to support Almira's younger sister Adelia by working as an embroiderer.[55]

Jackson and Almira settled in New York's Lower West Side - the area now encompassing SoHo, the South

---

49 "Base Ball and Skating", "The Brooklyn Daily Eagle", February 7, 1861
50 United States Census, 1850; New York State Census, 1855
51 "Another Case of Official Corruption: Judge Bogart Tried for Taking Straw Bail", February 7, 1856
52 "New York Daily Tribune", February 8, 1856
53 "Conviction of Justice Bogart for Misdemeanor", "The Brooklyn Daily Eagle", September 9, 1856
54 "Death of Ex-Police Justice Bogart", "The New York Times", November 22, 1856
55 1860 United States Census

Village and Hudson Square.[56] They had three children in quick succession, sons Abram and Eugene in 1859[57] and 1861 and daughter Clara Louise in 1862.[58] Almira was six years younger than Jackson, barely a teenager herself when their first child was born.[59] The couple moved at least four times in four years.[60]

With the Civil War on the horizon[61], New York theatre managers closed their doors one by one during the winter of 1860-61. These closures ultimately proved to be short-lived. When venues began re-opening, managers and playwrights alike recognized the marketability of entertainment based on real-life events. War tableaus, panoramas and dramatizations effectively became Union propaganda, and soon theatres were packed after victories and almost empty after defeats.[62] In the summer of 1861, the Winter Garden Theatre staged a patriotic drama based on The Battle of Fort Sumter.[63] It was "replete with stirring events of military

---

56 United States Census, 1860; "Early New York City Wards", The New York Genealogical and Biographical Society, 2016
57 New York, New York City Births, 1846-1909
58 New York State Census, 1865
59 New York State Census, 1855; New York, New York City Births, 1846-1909
60 Trow's New York City Directory, 1861-1864 (4 issues)
61 "A Short History of the Civil War", James L. Stokesbury, 2011
62 "A History of the American Drama", Arthur Hobson Quinn, 1936; "The Civil War from The New York Stage", Huber W. Ellingsworth, "Southern Speech Journal", Vol. 19, March 1954
63 "America's Dream at The Winter Garden", June 25, 1861; "The Civil War from The New York Stage", Huber W.

life, camp scenes [and] battle fields" called "America's Dream or The Rebellion of '61".[64]

On the opening night, Jackson brought much-needed levity to the production with his parlour skating performance.[65] The second night, he lost his balance and, unable to slow down, fell into the orchestra pit. It wasn't a tiny tumble either. He knocked over a gas lamp, injuring himself and several members of the orchestra. His blunder was unpopular with both the audience and the Winter Garden's Director. Though some regarded him as "a madman who wasted his time and ability on a foolish and unfeasible enterprise," he was completely undeterred in his pursuit to make something of himself as a parlour skater.[66]

W.H. Disbrow gave Jackson a job as a professor[67] at his Skating Gymnasium, where he gave a series of exhibitions in the autumn of 1861 to draw in patrons.[68] Advertisements from the Gymnasium read, "Open every

---

Ellingsworth, "Southern Speech Journal", Vol. 19, March 1954

64 Advertisements, "The New York Herald", July 26, 1861
65 "Laibacher Zeitung", October 31, 1867
66 "Der Schlittschuhläufer Haines", "Tagespost", August 17, 1867; "Tages-Post", December 31, 1871
67 "Jackson Haines, The Champion Skater Of The World", "The Illustrated Sporting News", September 17, 1864; Correspondence with the National Skating Association, George Henry Browne, 1891 and 1901, cited in "Ice Abroad: From The British Archives", Dennis L. Bird, "Skating" magazine, February 1978
68 Advertisements, "The New York Times", October 5, 1861

evening from 8 to 10 o'clock, for ladies, gentlemen and children for parlor-skating. Mr. J. Haines, professor of skating, will exhibit his unrivaled performance every evening."[69] Soon, Disbrow's Skating Gymnasium had competition from a similar establishment - Professor Bond's Dancing and Skating Academy on Varick Street, which offered instruction in "all the fashionable dances, and likewise the art of skating, taught in one course of lessons."[70]

During the winter of 1861-62, Jackson performed on parlour skates at Professor Trenor's Hall on South Eighth Street and on ice at the Van Rensselaer Skating Park in Albany[71] and the Union Skating Pond in Brooklyn[72].

Likely inspired by Jackson's performances accompanied by the music of a band, the latter skating pond installed a pagoda, housing a refreshment saloon and a thirty-five key contraption called a Strephilation, described as "an instrument on the same plan as a caliope, and is played in the same way, by steam."[73]

Jackson's evolutions to music were a revelation to the

---

69 Advertisements, "The New York Times", October 5, 1861
70 Advertisements, "New York Daily Herald", January 14, 1862
71 "News From The State Capital", "New York Daily Herald", January 30, 1862
72 "Skating", "Brooklyn Times Union", December 28, 1861
73 "Skating", "The Brooklyn Daily Eagle", December 30, 1861; "The Incoming Skating Season: The Skating Ponds in New-York, Brooklyn and Hoboken", "The New York Times", December 5, 1862

thousands that flocked to New York's skating ponds. Many tried to copy his style of skating, with little success. This beautifully penned description of one of his performances that winter captures the sense of awe his skating inspired: "A great attraction of the evening was Mr. Haines, who had engaged to be present. A crowd surrounded him during the whole evening, unless he ran away from it. The figures he made on the ice were surprising, and many an adventurer received a bumped head in trying to imitate him. Mr. H. had on a handsome pair of smooth-bottomed half rockers, screwed fast to a pair of shoes, and with no straps. He jumped on the ice, stamped to see that he was all right, then darted off like a whirlwind. He flung off half a dozen circles on the right leg, half a dozen with the left, and the same with either leg backwards. The ice traced with these white peripheries showed like a black board where a school had been chalking diagrams of Euclid... Mr. H. is a little man, all suppleness and activity. He is a magician on skates, and we can't describe him. A sheet of paper and a pen point can no more describe his movements than it can supply the place of a sheet of ice and keen skate edge. To skate forward and backward - to skate on the outer edge freely, to repeat pirouettes and spread eagles, to cross his feet, on the edge, forward and backward, and shift edge on the same foot, were but trifles to Haines. To those he added an indefinite list of combinations and fresh continuances. He spun spirals slow and spirals neck or nothing. He pivoted on one toe, with the other cutting rings, inner and outer edge, forward and back. He skated on one foot better than others could do on both. He ran on his toes; he slid on his heels; he danced; he waltzed; he cut up shines like a sunbeam on a bender; he swung, light as if he could fly, if he pleased, like a wing-footed Mercury; he glided as if will, not muscle, moved him; he tore about in frenzies; his pivotal leg stood firm; his balance leg flapped like a graceful pinion; he could write his name, podograph any letter and multitudes of ingenious curlicues, which might pass for the alphabets of unknown tongues."[74] Jackson's skating didn't only inspire awe. It was almost considered exotic.

---

[74] "On Ice", "Brooklyn Times Union", December 30, 1861

1. Avoid skates which are strapped on the feet, as they prevent the circulation, and the foot becomes frozen before the skater is aware of it, because the tight strapping benumbs the foot and deprives it of feeling. A young lady at Boston lost a foot in this way; another in New-York, her life, by endeavoring to thaw her feet in warm water, after taking off her skates. The safest kind are those which receive the fore-part of the foot in a kind of toe, and stout leather around the heel, buckling in front of the ankle only, thus keeping the heel in place without spikes or screws, and aiding greatly in supporting the ankle.

2. It is not the object so much to skate fast, as to skate gracefully; and this is sooner and more easily learned by skating with deliberation; while it prevents overheating, and diminishes the chances of taking cold by cooling off too soon afterward.

3. If the wind is blowing, a vail should be worn over the face, at least of ladies and children; otherwise, fatal inflammation of the lungs, "pneumonia," may take place.

4. Do not sit down to rest a single half-minute; nor stand still, if there is any wind; nor stop a moment after the skates are taken off; but walk about, so as to restore the circulation about the feet and toes, and to prevent being chilled.

5. It is safer to walk home than to ride; the latter is almost certain to give a cold.

6. Never carry any thing in the mouth while skating, nor any hard substance in the hand; nor throw any thing on the ice; none but a careless, reckless ignoramus, would thus endanger a *fellow*-skater a *fall*.

7. If the thermometer is below thirty, and the wind is blowing, no lady or child should be skating.

8. Always keep your eyes about you, looking ahead and upward, not on the ice, that you may not run against some lady, child, or learner.

9. Arrange to have an extra garment, thick and heavy, to throw over your shoulders, the moment you cease skating, and then walk home, or at least half a mile, with your mouth closed, so that the lungs may not be quickly chilled, by the cold air dashing upon them, through the open mouth; if it passes through the nose and head, it is warmed before it gets to the lungs.

10. It would be a safe rule for no child or lady to be on skates longer than an hour at a time.

11. The grace, exercise, and healthfulness of skating on the ice, can be had, without any of its dangers, by the use of skates with rollers attached, on common floors; better if covered with oil-cloth. Lessons are given in this pleasant and exhilarating exercise at Mr. Disbrow's on Fifth Avenue, whose spacious and well-conducted establishment ought to be well patronized.

Advice to skaters from "Hall's Journal of Health", 1860, mentioning Disbrow's Skating Gymnasium, where Jackson taught

By late March, the ice had melted. After an engagement at the Troy Gymnasium[75], Jackson appeared on parlour skates in a variety production touted as "Increased Attraction, More Novelty, More Brilliancy: Another Mammoth Programme" at the Great Canterbury Music Hall in New York.[76] He was engaged at the Holliday Street Theatre in Baltimore in June, performing on parlour skates during a double feature of "The Young Widow" and "Andy Blake".[77]

Theatrical productions in those days often had a Vaudeville or music hall flavour. A night out at the theatre would often consist of one or more plays, musicals, dance and minstrel show acts. It was in these 'variety show' type productions on parlour skates – not on the ice - that Jackson started making a name for himself. His performances were viewed as "a novelty in the way of amusement".[78]

In the summer of 1862, Jackson made his first of many appearances at Fox's Old Bowery Theatre in New York, performing during the burlesque play "King Cotton" and "The Head of The Family".[79] From August to October, he went on the road with Fox's Ravel Troupe, a travelling theatrical company who were one of the first such companies in America to prominently feature roller

---

75 "Troy Gymnasium", "Albany Morning Express", March 29, 1862
76 Advertisements, "New York Daily Herald", April 10, 1862
77 Advertisements, "The Baltimore Sun", June 20, 1862
78 "Chance Clippings", "The Chatham Courier", October 6, 1864
79 Advertisements, "Sunday Dispatch", July 20, 1862

skating.[80]

Jackson gave performances in Boston at The Howard Athenæum (Old Howard Theatre)[81], as well as in Springfield (Massachusetts)[82], Hartford[83], New Haven[84], Providence[85], Baltimore[86] and Philadelphia.[87] In November and December, he appeared on parlour skates at Green Street Varieties in Albany[88] and at the Pittsburgh Theatre, skating between performances of "Peep o' Day Boys" and "Deeds of a Dreadful Nature".[89]

During the winter of 1862-63, Jackson performed on parlour skates as a novelty during numerous plays at Fox's Old Bowery Theatre, including "Jack and the Beanstalk"[90], "Wandering Steenie or The Bridal of the

---

80 "Haines the Skater", "Troy Daily Times", January 24, 1873
81 "Fox's Ravel Troupe!: first appearance of the celebrated Annetta Galletti! ... August 4, 1862", Broadside in the Boston Athenæum Digital Collections; "Third week of the continued success of the great and unrivalled pantomimists, Fox's Ravel Troupe", playbill, American Antiquarian Society, August 4, 1862
82 Advertisements, "New York Clipper", September 13, 1862
83 "Hartford Courant", September 22, 1862
84 Advertisements, "New York Clipper", September 13, 1862
85 Advertisements, "Providence Evening Press", September 1, 1862
86 "Miscellaneous", "New York Clipper", October 11, 1862
87 Advertisements, "New York Clipper", October 18, 1862
88 Advertisements, "Albany Morning Express", December 4, 1863
89 Advertisements, "The Pittsburgh Gazette", December 2, 1862
90 Advertisements, "New York Daily Herald", January 9, 1863'

Borders", "Mother Goose and the Golden Egg" and "Wardock Kennilson or The Woman of the Village".[91] In between performances, he obtained bookings on the ice in skating carnivals in New York City, Rochester and Buffalo[92]. During practices in Buffalo, he fell and severely injured his shoulder, rendering him "unable to perform many of his most difficult evolutions."[93]

In March, Jackson headed North to Toronto for a few weeks. He gave lessons to Canadian skaters and performed a series of exhibitions on the city's outdoor skating ponds. On the evening he left, he penned the following letter to the editor of "The Globe"[94]:

Sir - Before leaving your beautiful city I thought it would be nothing less than my duty to give to your citizens the benefit of my experience with regard to the manner of keeping their skating 'rinks' or ponds in the most healthful and beneficial condition. I have no doubt that skating will be the rage next winter to a greater extent than it has been this.

I have been told that the proprietors of some of the ponds intend covering them to avoid the effects of the sun and the inconvenience of snow. This will be found very injurious to health, particularly

---

"The age and stage of George L. Fox, 1825-1877", Laurence Senelick, 1988
91 Advertisements, "The New York Herald", February 15, 1863
92 "New York Clipper", January 3, 1863; "Local News", "Buffalo Evening Post", January 21, 1863
93 "The Skating Exhibition", "Buffalo Morning Express", March 9, 1863
94 "Haines Preferred Open Rinks", John S. MacLean, "Skating" magazine, March 1946

of children, whose lungs are more active and require more ventilation and fresh air than adults. The experiment has been tried in New York and abandoned. The ice on an open rink, when exposed to all the effects of nature, is found to be much more pleasant to skate upon and no matter how well the house may be ventilated a certain degree of dampness will be retained under the cover, that has been found exceedingly injurious to persons of tender years. Skating is a violent exercise, and a person when under such excitement needs all the pure, healthful air that it is possible to have. Hoping that this may not be unacceptable to your readers I remain the well-wisher of Toronto.

JACKSON HAINES,
Prof. of Skating.

Toronto, March 24, 1863

From March to December of 1863, Jackson continued to 'sing for his supper' as an itinerant stage performer, giving a dizzying series of performances. He appeared on his parlour skates in New York City at Fox's Old Bowery Theatre[95], the New Bowery Theatre[96], Hooley's Opera House[97] and George Christy's Minstrels[98] on Broadway, in Albany at the Green Street Theatre[99], in Philadelphia at the Continental Theatre on Walnut

---

95 Advertisements, "New York Herald", April 21, 1863
96 Advertisements, "The New York Herald", October 29, 1863
97 "Hooley's Opera House", "The Brooklyn Daily Eagle", October 22, 1863
98 Advertisements, "The New York Herald", October 31, 1863
99 Advertisements, "New York Clipper", November 28, 1863

Street[100], in Boston at Morris Brother's Pell & Trowbridge's Opera House and Buffalo at St. James Hall.[101]

It was just the beginning.

---

[100] Advertisements, "New York Clipper", May 23, 1863
[101] Advertisements, "Buffalo Evening Post", March 14, 1863

1864

In the winter of 1863-1864, Jackson set out on what may well be considered North America's first true 'one man show' ice skating tour. Billed as "The Great American Skater", he performed on the skating ponds of Boston, Brooklyn, Utica[102], Syracuse[103], Rochester[104], Buffalo, Chicago[105], Detroit[106], London[107], Hamilton[108], Toronto[109], Kingston[110], Brockville[111], Ottawa[112],

---

[102] "Theatrical Record", "New York Clipper", January 16, 1864
[103] "Theatrical Record", "New York Clipper", January 16, 1864
[104] "Theatrical Record", "New York Clipper", January 16, 1864
[105] Advertisements, "Chicago Tribune", January 23, 1864
[106] "The Champion Skater and his Exhibition at the Third Street Park", "Detroit Free Press", February 4, 1864
[107] "The London Free Press & Daily Western Advertiser", February 10, 1864
[108] "Skating", "The Hamilton Times", February 13, 1864
[109] "The Champion Skater", "The Daily Globe", February 16, 1864
[110] "Skating", "The Daily News", February 26, 1864; "The Rinks and Rinkists of Kingston", Bill Fitsell, "Historic Kingston", Vol. 34, 1986
[111] "Mr. Jackson Haines", "The Daily British Whig", February 26, 1864
[112] "Local News", "Ottawa Daily Citizen", March 4, 1864

Montreal[113] and Quebec City.[114]

Without his skates on, Jackson was only five feet, four inches,[115] but on the ice he had a commanding presence which belied his stature. In his performances, he demonstrated an adeptness at carving out the 'fancy' or special figures which were so popular at the time. One witness to his skating raved that he "exhibited some of the finest 'cuts' imaginable, in his flights across the smooth surface - making figures of birds and beasts, of houses and of forests - to the delight of all."[116] Another highlight of Jackson's performances was a spin of his own invention, termed in the 1860s as the "One-Foot Spin, peculiar" and later simply called the Jackson Haines Spin. In 1868, journalist Marvin R. Clark and William H. Bishop (stage name Frank Swift) described it thusly: "This world-renowned skater's great specialty is, doing a 'one-foot' spin,' and while revolving, stooping so low that his balance leg must necessarily be horizontal to clear the ice, then rising gradually and finishing the spin upon his toe."[117] It was said that the spin took Jackson many years to master. This spin ultimately devolved from what was essentially a spin combination[118] into the

---

113 "Jackson Haines, Célèbre Patineur", "Le Pays", March 10, 1864
114 "Miscellaneous", "New York Clipper", March 26, 1864
115 United States Passport Application of Jackson Haines, July 2, 1864
116 "Skating", "The Brooklyn Daily Eagle", December 30, 1861
117 "Specialties of Prominent Skaters", "The Skaters Text Book", Marvin R. Clark and William H. Bishop (Frank Swift), 1868
118 "Skøiteløberkunsten, fremstillet med Figurerne in Jsen", Thorwald Groth, 1882

modern-day sit spin.

The 'One-Foot Spin, peculiar' wasn't Jackson's only technical innovation. He was often known "to lean backwards while skating backwards, till his hair touches the ice, and then, without help, recover a perpendicular position."[119] The description of this movement evokes to mind the Cantilever back-end, a trick later performed to great effect in ice revues.

An account of one of Jackson's Canadian performances raved, "Mr. Haines, though not a large or muscular man, is compactly built, and appeared on the ice in a neatly-fitted jacket, and wearing a gold medal presented to him by the Chicago Board of Trade, as a mark of esteem and admiration for his skill in the skating art. Accompanied by the Fife and Drum band of the 63rd regiment, Haines danced a highland fling in capital style. He also danced a difficult clog hornpipe, and a slow waltz, together with several other dances. After this, the champion dashed forward and by a singularly expert whirl spun around, dropping at an angle of forty-five degrees. The next figures were the forward and backward spiral movement, the sewing stitch, and the double grape vine twist, the cross back roll, double cross back roll and a number of other superb movements... Jackson Haines is one of the greatest skaters in the world, and thoroughly deserves public attention and support." Of note is the fact that Haines was presented a medal in Chicago as a "token of esteem". The actual

---

119 "Foreign", "Frank Leslie's Illustrated Newspaper", April 15, 1865

inscription on the medal read, "Presented to Jackson Haines, as a token of esteem and admiration for his skill in the art of skating. Chicago, January 30, 1864." Medals he received in Chicago and Quebec used the terms "esteem" and "admiration" as well.[120]

During the 1860s and 1870s, fancy skating competitions generally came about when skaters wrote into a newspaper challenging a rival to meet them and compete for a cash prize. No governing body existed to 'rule the roost' at that time. Any city could claim that the best skater in whatever they decided to call their competition was the American, Canadian or World Champion. Jackson may very well have been named 'the champion skater of America', but primary sources simply don't back up the traditional story of him winning a 'Championships Of America' in 1864 in Albany, New York City, Troy, Chicago or Detroit, as varying biographies over the years have claimed. Though he was challenged to do so at least three times[121], there is no evidence of him ever entering any skating competition in North America.

Jackson was particularly well-received during the Canadian stops on his skating tour. He was invited back to Montreal to give a series of performances on parlour

---

[120] "Jackson Haines, The Champion Skater Of The World", "The Illustrated Sporting News", September 17, 1864

[121] "The Skating Season", "Brooklyn Daily Eagle", February 5, 1863; "The City and Vicinity", "The Daily Courier", January 14, 1864; "Skating - Jackson Haines", "Chicago Tribune", February 4, 1864

skates at Joseph Édouard Guilbault's Botanic and Zoological Gardens in July of 1864 after giving his last American performances in conjunction with minstrel shows in Boston.[122], Chicago[123] and Albany.[124] The Jardin Guilbault productions[125] would be his last performances on the Continent. At the age of twenty-six, he boarded a ship in Boston on August 17, 1864[126], never to be seen in North America again.

Before we take a deep dive into Jackson's adventures in Europe, it is essential to follow the paper trail to get a sense of why he went there in the first place. It has been said that his parents wanted him to go in the family business, but he hated working in an office and wanted to skate instead.[127] This may have been true, as Census records do suggest that he had ties to his father's fruit business[128], but he was never home in New York long enough to have worked there full-time.

A folktale, repeated time and time again, was that Jackson left because his talents were not appreciated in North America.[129] This couldn't have been farther from

---

[122] "Miscellaneous", "New York Clipper", May 14, 1864
[123] Advertisements, "Chicago Daily Tribune", June 12, 1864
[124] Amusements, "Albany Morning Express", July 8, 1864
[125] "Nouvelles du Canada", "La Minerve", July 16, 1864
[126] "Miscellaneous", "New York Clipper", August 27, 1864; "Jackson Haines, The Champion Skater Of The World", "The Illustrated Sporting News", September 17, 1864
[127] "Nya Dagligt Allehanda" (Stockholm), June 25, 1875
[128] 1860 United States Census
[129] "The Man Who Invented Figure Skating Was Laughed Out of America", Erin Blakemore, History Channel blog, December

the truth. He gave dozens upon dozens of performances in the United States and Canada and received nothing but effusive praise at the time. This description of his skating, penned by a Chicago reporter, was one of dozens of similarly glowing articles: "Jackson Haines is a young, fair-looking and gracefully-formed man, with splendidly developed muscles, and as lithe and agile as a cat. Strength, as well as activity, and a philosophical knowledge of equilibrium, enter into the performance of his feats, to which must be added a most wonderful grace. His rolls forward and backward, which best attest the excellence of the skater, seem to us perfection. Any person who can skate can skate very fast, and this very properly is considered but a second-rate element in skating. Grace is the principal feature, and in this element Haines excels. The most graceful of danseuses who has flung herself across the stage might well sigh for the symmetrical curves and poises which one like Haines can attain on the narrow rim of steel... Elasticity and strength of ankle, the suppleness and agility of the acrobat and symmetrical grace, surpassing the best dancers, are the elements which enter into the rendition of these feats, and form a picture worth the studying of any one who delights in witnessing the highest accomplishments of the human figure."[130] There was a world of opportunity for him to showcase his skating to new audiences abroad, but he was certainly not unappreciated in North America.

12, 2017

[130] "Jackson Haines and The Poetry of Skating", "Chicago Tribune", January 23, 1864

Jackson announced his intention to leave for Europe as early as March of 1863[131], well before he went on his ice skating tour of North America. By that June, he had been enumerated for the draft to serve in the Civil War.[132] Over twenty percent of those who were drafted to serve in the Civil War refused to report for duty or went into hiding to avoid the provost marshals. It is certainly unusual that there is no record of Jackson performing in the state of New York, where he was drafted, after January of 1864. All but two of the venues where he performed during the last months he was in North America were in Canada.

There is room for speculation that Jackson may have left the United States with a false passport in his possession. He applied for his own on July 2, 1864[133] and travelled under his own name when he left the United States.[134] However, a lost trunk of his possessions, found at the state railway station in Budapest in 1871, contained the passport of a dancer named Jones,[135] and an article published shortly after his death in Vienna stated that he

---

[131] "The City and Vicinity", "Evening Courier & Republic", March 14, 1863

[132] Schedule I - Consolidated List of all persons of Class I, subject to do military duty in the Fourteenth Congressional District (Records of the Provost Marshal General's Bureau, 1863-1865)

[133] United States Passport Application of Jackson Haines, July 2, 1864

[134] "Arrival of the Africa: List of Passengers", "Liverpool Daily Post", August 30, 1864

[135] "Neues Fremden-Blatt", May 3, 1871

was also known by the name Cornac Jones.[136] This may have been an alias. There is no record of any United States passport being issued to anyone with the name Cornac Jones from 1864 to 1871.

The biggest curiosity about Jackson's departure involves his family. On August 1, he went before Justice Barnard of the New York Supreme Court, initiating what appeared to be divorce proceedings against Almira. The Judge ruled that the "defendant [was] allowed to come in and defend on consenting to refer. If defendant so elects, $25 allowed for counsel fee, and $3 week per alimony."[137] There is no record of these proceedings developing any further[138] because Jackson left the country. In those days, divorce was extremely taboo, so this may or may not have played some role in Jackson and/or Almira's decision not to pursue the matter further in the courts.[139]

Jackson's departure for Europe without a divorce or alimony finalized left Almira in an impossible financial situation. Essentially destitute, she was forced to leave Abram, Eugene and Clara Louise in the care of

---

136 "Wiener Theater-Chronik", July 9, 1875
137 "Supreme Court - Chambers - Aug. 1 - Before Justice Barnard", "New York Daily Tribune", August 2, 1864
138 Correspondence with Joseph Van Nostrand, Division of Old Records, New York State Unified Court System, March 7, 2023
139 "Divorce and Custody", Mary Ann Mason, "The Encyclopedia of Children and Childhood in History and Society", 2008

Jackson's parents.[140]

The Royal Mail Steamship Africa

Two days after boarding the Royal Mail Steamship Africa in Boston on August 17, 1864[141], Jackson arrived in Halifax, Nova Scotia for a short stop before making the Atlantic passage. The Africa was the fourth-largest ship in the Cunard Fleet at the time[142], capable of carrying up to one hundred and eighty passengers[143], but it was only just over half full during Jackson's voyage.[144]

During the first part of Jackson's Transatlantic passage, the Africa encountered a dangerous south-easterly gale

---

140 "Suit For The Possession Of A Child", "Daily Albany Argus", September 19, 1871
141 "Passengers", "Boston Daily Advertiser", August 17, 1864
142 "The Cunard Fleet", "Liverpool Transcript", August 25, 1864
143 Norway Heritage Project, Børge Solem
144 "Federal Shipping", "Liverpool Mercury", August 29, 1864

that brought harrowing winds, pelting rain and choppy seas. Once the ship made it through the storm, the Captain had to contend with dense fog. After nine long days at sea, the Africa made a brief stop in Queenstown, Ireland before arriving in Liverpool, England on August 29, 1864.[145]

Jackson made his way south to London, where an agent he had secured in Boston had arranged daily bookings at The Crystal Palace in Hyde Park and Cremorne Gardens in Chelsea. He performed on a platform in front of the Shakespeare House, on a double-bill with a young tightrope walker who went by the stage name Le Petit Blondin[146], after the famous French acrobat Charles Blondin.[147] The well-to-do Victorians, who called his conveyance 'drawing-room skates', were delighted by his performances. A report in the "Sun" remarked, "Mr. Jackson Haines, the champion skater of America, is now performing at the Crystal Palace, and yesterday drew a goodly number to witness his very graceful performance. He performs on a skate with three or four India-rubber wheels at the bottom, and goes through a series of dances. He moves with great rapidity, and indeed, his performance is one of the prettiest imaginable."[148] Artemas Ward, a popular American humourist staying in England at the time, hailed him as

---

[145] "Arrival of the Africa", "Sheffield and Rotherham Independent", August 30, 1864
[146] Advertisements, "Morning Herald", September 26, 1864
[147] "The Daredevil of Niagara Falls", "Smithsonian" magazine, Karen Abbott, October 18, 2011
[148] "Crystal Palace", "Sun", September 27, 1864

"The Great Skatist of the Age".[149]

In between performances, Jackson called at the office of the Minister of the Court of St. James's. Secretary Benjamin Moran wrote of Jackson in his journal: "A sharp little fellow calling himself Jackson Haines, a man who has been lately giving exhibitions in skating in London, called today. He is not more than 5 ft. 4 - slender and yet compact... He told me he was born in New York. From all I can hear he has made quite a sensation in London and is... going to Russia."[150]

Jackson's 'spread-eagles' and 'figures of eight' at the Cremorne Gardens and Crystal Palace led to a three-month engagement with the Oxford and Canterbury Hall Company[151], followed by a stint at Weston's Music Hall in Holborn.[152] His quick success in London must have come as a considerable surprise. On November 17, 1864, he sent a letter and photograph to a Paris newspaper stating his intention to come perform there the following week, but was such a draw in England he was forced to delay his trip to France.[153]

---

149 Advertisements, "London Evening Standard", October 2, 1869
150 November 9, 1864 entry, "The Journal of Benjamin Moran, 1857-1865", Volume 2, edited by Sarah Agnes Wallace and Frances Elma Gillespie, 1948
151 "The Oxford Company", "London Evening Standard", November 12, 1864
152 "Weston's Music Hall, Holborn", "Morning Advertiser", December 6, 1864
153 "Paris", "Le Petit Journal", November 22, 1864

46

Jackson's performances on 'drawing-room skates' were a prominent feature of the Crystal Palace's Christmas Holiday Amusements.[154] During Christmas Week of 1864, he was said to have been invited to perform before The Royal Family at Windsor Castle,[155] but there is no record of any such performance actually taking place in Her Majesty Queen Victoria's journal or the index of the Royal Archives.[156]

---

[154] "Going To The Play", "Penny Illustrated Paper", January 7, 1865
[155] "Jackson Haines", "Chicago Tribune", January 21, 1865
[156] Correspondence with Colin Parrish, Research Room and Enquires Assistant at Royal Archives, Private Secretary's Office, Windsor Castle, February 28, 2023

49

1865

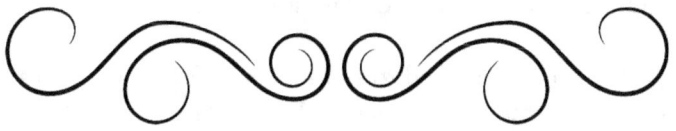

After the holiday shows at the Crystal Palace drew to a close in early January, Jackson made his first of many passages to the Continent. Transportation in Europe at the time was a far cry from what it is today. Getting from point A to point B would often involve multiple modes of transport - ships, steam locomotives and horse-drawn carriages or carts.

Jackson first travelled to Paris, making stops in Rotterdam and Amsterdam.[157] Back home in New York, the newspapers reported, "This splendid skater has not only attracted great attention in England and France by his skill on skates, but he has found his visit to be particularly beneficial to him, inasmuch as he realized over £1,000 sterling in England and 10,000f. in France. His appearance on the Serpentine river in Hyde Park attracted such crowds on the ice that the police had to interfere to prevent the ice from giving way. He found no one to surpass him in England, but in France he met a competitor worthy of his steel an agile Frenchman - whose skill as a practised acrobat in one of the circus companies of Paris, combined with his grace of movement on skates, led to Haines having to yield the

---

[157]"Jackson Haines", "Chicago Tribune", January 21, 1865

palm."[158] Curiously, no record of any such contest appears in French newspapers or magazines, but interestingly, Paris' famous Cercle des Patineurs was founded the same year of Jackson's visit.[159]

Jackson next ventured to Berlin, where he gave a series of three exhibitions on ice at the Tiergarten-Eisbahn before over ten thousand paying spectators. He also performed during a snowstorm at an 'Eispartie' near Rousseau Island, accompanied by music especially composed for him by the Austrian Grenadier Regiment.[160] A report of the latter performance raved, "A number of the royal princes, many court gentlemen and ladies were assembled to witness the performance. Mr. Haines was attired in a tight dark suit, and on his breast wore the medals... [from] Chicago, New York and other American cities. The lightning rapidity, the elegance and the grace of all his movements threw the whole public into astonishment. The skill and ease with which he drew the most difficult devices on the ice were, according to the judgment of his Berlin critics, something almost incredible. He seemed to engrave with his feet."[161] Jackson also demonstrated his skill on his parlour skates at the Victoria-Theater at Münzstrasse 20. Among his performances was his signature "Le Novice", a program parodying a beginner skater he had used to

---

158 "Jackson Haines, Europe", "Brooklyn Daily Eagle", January 31, 1865
159 "Les Sports d'Hiver", Louis Magnus, 1911
160 "Albany Express", March 1, 1865
161 "Our Editorial Sanctum", "Gazlay's Pacific Monthly", January-June 1865, Vol. I

great effect in his North American and British shows.[162]

The success of Jackson's performances in the Deutscher Bund resulted in his first of many trips to the Russian Empire in February, performing first in St. Petersburg, then in Moscow. His theatrical style of skating, heavy on pose, was extremely well-received by the ballet-loving Russians, who had just formed their first skating club approximately two years prior.[163] Vyacheslav Sreznevsky, a witness of one of Jackson's first performances in St. Petersburg, later remarked, "The skating of Haines seemed to Russian skaters somehow a revelation: the amazing ease and ease of performing very complex figures, the extraordinary grace of movements left an indelible impression on the audience."[164] His performances also made quite an impression on the oligarchy. Czar Alexander II, the Emperor of Russia, King of Poland and Grand Duke of Finland, gave him "a very handsome ring, with a ruby centre and five first-water diamonds on either side." Grand Duke Konstantin Nikolayevich, the Viceroy of the Kingdom of Poland, presented him "with a beautiful medal [with] a very large circle of Siberian crystal, in which are set letters of gold, stating the object of the gift. The edge is of solid gold,

---

162 "Die Auftritte des amerikanischen 'Schlittschuhkünstlers' Jackson Haines in Deutschland", Dr. Matthias Hampe, "Pirouette" magazine, February 2019; "Jackson Haines – der amerikanische Schlittschuhkünstler", "Illustrirte Zeitung", February 11, 1865

163 "A Winter At St. Petersburg", "London Society", Volume 11, January 1867

164 "Skating rink on Petrovka, 26: The history of the first Moscow club of figure skating", Yuri Yakimchuk, 2006

and it is surmounted with gold straps, dotted with rubies and pearls."[165] He also received a gold and diamond medal from the Navy Club of Kronstadt[166] after accepting an invitation to perform by the American Consul. In St. Petersburg, an American flag was installed atop a small hut set up on the ice for him to change in.[167]

In April, news reached Europe of the surrender of Confederate Army General Robert E. Lee to Union Army Ulysses S. Grant, signalling an end to the Civil War and President Abraham Lincoln's assassination by Confederate sympathizer John Wilkes Booth.[168] The unrest in America and its impact on Jackson's family back home would have undoubtedly weighed heavily on his mind.

Jackson returned to England in June[169], giving a series of exhibitions on his 'drawing-room skates' at the Royal Alhambra Theatre in London. Henry Eugene Vandervell and T. Maxwell Witham, two eminent English Style skaters of the era, remarked, "Haines, the so-called 'champion skater', performed some wonderful feats on mechanical skates, but it was apparent that he did all his

---

165 "Troy Weekly Times", July 8, 1865
166 "Jackson Haines", "The Marysville Daily Appeal", August 16, 1865
167 "Summary of News", "The Philadelphia Inquirer", April 5, 1865
168 "Ending The Bloodshed: The Last Surrenders of the Civil War", Trevor K. Plante, National Archives, "Prologue magazine", Spring 2015, Vol. 47, No. 1
169 Advertisements, "Morning Advertiser", June 20, 1865

performance with great exertion to himself."[170]

Jackson spent three months in Birmingham performing at Day's Concert Hall and the Prince of Wales Theatre before returning to the Crystal Palace in London. Billed as "The Champion Skater of the World"[171], he was praised as "the incarnation of gracefulness upon skates."[172] An elaborate stage set was designed, resembling a frozen lake, to create the illusion that he was performing on ice and not rollers.[173] He performed one of his signature programs, an interpretation of the half-witted aristocrat Lord Dundreary, from British playwright Tom Taylor's production "Our American Cousin". This comedic program was received with "screams of laughter nightly".[174] The Lord Dundreary character was an ironic choice for an American travelling abroad, as it was during a presentation of "Our American Cousin" that President Lincoln had been killed just months prior.[175]

Jackson was met in England by his agent, Dr. Spear from Boston, who brought with him "a full-length landscape

---

170 "A System of Figure-Skating: The Theory and Practice as Developed in England", Henry Eugene Vandervell and Thomas Maxwell Witham, 1869 (1st edition)
171 Advertisements, "Sporting Life", June 21, 1865
172 "London Music Halls", "The Era", July 16, 1865
173 "Provincial Theatricals", "The Era", October 29, 1865
174 Advertisements, "Aris's Birmingham Gazette", August 19, 1865
175 "The Ford Theatre Lincoln assassination play-bill, Friday evening, April 14, 1865, Our American Cousin", Library of Congress

likeness of Jackson, skating, in a uniform trimmed with Russian furs" to advertise his appearances. This piece was painted by an Albany artist named Mr. Francois and "intended as a gift to the skating society of Neva, Russia, whose President, the Grand Duke [Konstantin] has been a liberal patron of the young American."[176] The theatrical novelty of Jackson's skating, coupled with this full-length landscape, would have seemed like imagination brought to life to the British people, who were entranced by a new book that had just been published – Lewis Carroll's "Alice in Wonderland".[177]

---

176 "Jackson Haines", "Detroit Free Press", October 23, 1865
177 "Alice in Wonderland", National Library of Scotland

MR JACKSON HAINES THE CHAMPION SKATER, AT THE CRYSTAL PALACE

1866

Jackson returned to Russia, performing on the ice in the Garden of the Hermitage in Moscow[178] and on the frozen Neva River in St. Petersburg.

Chaos ensued at one performance in St. Petersburg, held during Maslenitsa celebrations. A report from a British correspondent in St. Petersburg recalled, "Notwithstanding the frost, which set in with unusual severity after a long continuance of mild weather, the pleasure-seekers were in a fever of excitement from Sunday to Sunday. The theatres, at all of which there were performances twice a day, were always full. There were luncheons, dinners, evening parties, or balls all over the town in every class of society, and the lower orders thronged the shows and theatres which offer attractive entertainments for every variety of taste. There were lion tamers, learned elephants, and boa constrictors, Aztecs and mermaids, to say nothing of the wonderful dramatic performances of horses and dogs, men and monkeys. For those who were actively disposed there were roundabouts and ice hills. Everything passed off very quietly with the exception of the performance of Jackson Haines, the American skater, on the first day of

---

178 "From Russia", "New York Tribune", February 10, 1866

the Carnival. After going through his evolutions for ten minutes he made his bow, but as this was at the rate of about a penny a minute the peasants thought it was hardly fair, and as Mr. Haines refused to come out again the mob began to pull down his booth, and the great skater would have been in a very awkward predicament if the police had not promptly interfered."[179] Threats were shouted and chairs and barriers were broken.[180] It is a reasonable supposition that the custom art piece Dr. Spear brought with him may have been damaged in the melee.

Leaving the Russians to their forty-day fast for the Eastern Orthodox Church's Great Lent[181], Jackson travelled to Latvia, where he gave several exhibitions in Mitau (Jelgava) and Riga.[182] To protect against the wind, a fenced rink was constructed especially for him on the frozen Düna River. Years later, the son of a local skater who saw Jackson's performances recalled, "The response was enormous, because the whole of Riga was enthusiastic about the phenomenal ice artist. To this day I can still see the slender man in his short black coat trimmed with light fur, a small fur beret and high lace-up boots hovering over the ice surface with tremendous momentum, infallible security and the most beautiful posture as he was drawing his huge figures in the ice. He attempted spirals, brilliant acrobatics and gliding edges,

---

179 "Russia", "London Evening Standard", March 1, 1866
180 "Rigasche Zeitung", February 9, 1866
181 "Russia", "London Evening Standard", March 1, 1866
182 "Rigasche Zeitung", February 15, 1866; "Rigasche Zeitung", February 28, 1866; "Revalsche Zeitung", February 9, 1874

even on one foot, forwards and backwards in conjunction with threes. Loops and pirouettes took up the entire spacious rink: one man filled it completely."

While in Riga, Jackson also made several visits to the Rosenbachshe Bahn on the Karlspfortenbassin, a winter camp organized by the proprietor of the local floating baths. There, he taught skating to several enthusiastic local skaters, mostly men between the ages of twenty and fifty. This group of men were regarded as Riga's figure skating pioneers – and they impersonated Jackson's style long after he left.[183]

Jackson travelled via Hamburg to Sweden in late March of 1866[184] and immediately procured a Russian-style costume. He headed out on the frozen Nybroviken Bay in Stockholm to show off his skills on a day that he knew that King Carl, his family and attendants would be on the ice. That afternoon, the King's Adjutant showed up at his hotel, inviting him to an audience at the Royal Court the next morning.[185]

As word of Jackson's royal audience in Russia spread like wildfire, skeptics who thought him "bold enough to come here to show the Stockholmers how to skate"[186]

---

183 "Rigasche Zeitung", December 29, 1922
184 "Rigasche Zeitung", February 28, 1866; "Norrköpings Tidningar", March 29, 1866
185 Letter from Jackson Haines to Andrew J. Dupignac, President of the New York Skating Club, cited in "The Ice King", "Evening Telegram", November 13, 1871
186 "Morning Herald", September 6, 1866

quickly changed their tune after watching his evolutions. Six hundred people paid admission[187] to see him skate, and a high fence was erected under a bridge to keep out looky-loos who didn't cough up the fee. There was such curiosity about Jackson's skating that "a lot of boys... climbed rather high rocks on the ends of the bridge" to be able to catch a glimpse of his performances without paying. He performed four numbers (a waltz, march, polka and mazurka) and was praised as "a premium ice dancer who showed elegance, agility and strength in his movements. There is something in his demeanour, truly graceful, which is enhanced by his pained figures and elegant attire... After each number, the artist was called out [to do] a number of pirouettes, which gave the people so much pleasure."[188]

In the months that followed, Jackson appeared on his parlour skates in conjunction with a French ballet company at the Teatern i Manegen[189] during a circus in the Djurgården[190] in Stockholm, the Nya Teatern in Gothenburg[191] and Kungliga Stora Theatern (Royal Opera House) in Stockholm.[192]

Jackson arrived in Denmark that autumn, shortly after

---

187 "Sundsvallsposten", April 7, 1866
188 "Den amerikanske skridskoåkaren", "Aftonbladet", March 31, 1866
189 Advertisements, "Nya Dagligt Allehanda", June 8, 1866
190 "Blekingsposten", June 5, 1866
191 "Halmstadbladet", August 10, 1866
192 "Offentliga Nöjen", "Post-Och Inrikes Tidningar", September 29, 1866

the announcement of the engagement of Princess Dagmar and Grand Duke Alexander, who later reigned as the Emperor of Russia.[193] He made his debut at the Kasino-Theater in Copenhagen on October 15. One Danish writer who saw his first performance was so moved by the "beautiful spectacle of his admirable skill and of the endearing elegance with which he moves" that they suggested "every lady and gentleman of the world should be as proficient at skating [as they are at studying] foreign languages... music and painting."[194]

Jackson returned to Stockholm in late November[195], resuming performances at the Kungliga Stora Theatern.[196] When the Nybroviken Bay was sufficiently frozen in December, he gave exhibitions on the ice and offered lessons to men, women and children.[197]

---

193 "Kejserinde Dagmar og musikken", Royal Danish Library
194 "Fædrelandet", October 16, 1866
195 "Göteborgsposten", November 29, 1866
196 "Norrköpings Tidningar", December 6, 1866
197 Advertisements, "Aftonbladet", December 22, 1866; Advertisements, "Nya Dagligt Allehanda", December 24, 1866, "Der Schlittschuhläufer Haines", "Tagespost", August 17, 1867

When Jackson was busy performing in Scandinavia, family weighed heavily on his mind. He sent a letter to his sister Elizabeth, asking her to come to Europe, with the idea they might skate together.[198]

Things weren't exactly rosy back at home. Jackson's parents had left New York City and followed their eldest son upstate. Eugene worked as a photographer[199] in the Troy and Albany areas. Jackson's parents, children and

---

198 "The Father of Figure Skating", Winfield A. Hird, "Skating" magazine, January 1941
199 New York State Census, 1865

sisters first settled in Lansingburgh and later rented a house with an orchard on Haver (Peebles) Island.[200] It wasn't long before the family found themselves at the center of a scandal. On August 8, the "Lansingburgh Weekly Chronicle" reported, "On Thursday of last week, a gentleman and lady, named William H. Bates and Almira Haines, of New York City, arrived in the 'Burgh and engaged rooms at the Phoenix Hotel, for the ostensible purpose of making a short sojourn in the 'Garden,' and which they did, as the sequel will show. The lady referred to proved to be the wife of Jackson Haines, the celebrated skater, who is now astonishing the crowned heads of Europe by his consummate skill as a skater, and whose father... resides in Lansingburgh. Previous to her husband's departure for Europe, his father, who was then a resident of New York city, who was appointed guardian for the children, consisting of three in number, and they were accordingly placed in his custody, as such guardian, for the purposes for which he was appointed, and upon his removal from New York he brought the children with him to Lansingburgh, as it would appear, without the consent of Mrs. Haines, their mother, but on the contrary against her will. Such at least was her statement. The mother, desirous to regain the custody of her children, came to Lansingburgh for

---

200 "At The Junction of the Hudson and the Mohawk: Archeological Excavation of a Late 18th-Century Site on Peebles Island, Peebles Island State Park, Waterford, Saratoga County, New York", Paul R. Huey, 2016; Account Book, Collection of the Lansingburgh Historical Society, A.A. Peebles, M.L.P. Peebles Records, Box 16. On deposit, Rensselaer County Historical Society

that purpose, and instead of proceeding in a legitimate way to obtain such custody, resulted in the arrest of both herself and her escort, Mr. Bates. Some time prior to the afternoon of Friday last, the parties called at the residence of [Alexander] Haines, apparently for the purpose of seeing the children and having an interview with them, the real object of the visit undoubtedly being to inspect the premises and decide upon [?] plan by which the custody of the children could be obtained. This belief is deduced from what subsequently transpired. Upon the Friday afternoon referred to, between four and five o'clock, Mr. Bates and Mrs. Haines were seen in the rear of Mr. [Alexander] Haines' residence, by some factory girls who were employed in an adjacent building. The latter was leading two of the children toward the Phoenix Hotel, where she succeeded in conveying them. As soon as this fact came to the knowledge of Mr. Haines, he proceeded to the hotel and demanded the children and the mother refused to surrender them - whereupon Mr. H. procured a warrant for the arrest of Mrs. Haines and her accomplice, Mr. Bates, on the charge of kidnapping. Officer Longstaff served the process, and the parties were arraigned before Justice Hearman for an examination, who, in consequence of the late hour in the day, declined to hear the same at that time, and bail was required for the appearance of the parties before Justice Lansing on the following day, Saturday, or by failure to procure said bail, be committed until such time. The re-delivery of the children into the custody of Mr. Haines was accepted as a sufficient recognizance, and the parties were held to await the determination of the following day's examination.

At two o'clock P. M. on Saturday the parties appeared, Justice Lansing's Court, Francis Rising, Esq., appeared for the people, and James R. Stevens, Esq., as counsel for the prisoners. Several witnesses were examined on the part of the prosecution, and after the testimony was all in, the counsel for the prisoners moved for their discharge, on the ground that the evidence did not sustain the charge of kidnapping; that if they were guilty of any crime at all, it was one entirely distinct from that with which the prisoners were charged, and upon which they were arrested. The Court took half an hour to examine the law, and being convinced that the evidence did not sustain the charge of kidnapping, discharged the prisoners, who returned to New York on the same evening."[201]

While Jackson was overseas being hailed as The Skating King, the Haines family would continue to be plagued by troubles... and The Skating King was powerless to change the chain of events he set in motion by leaving his family behind.

---

[201] "Arrested on the Charge of Kidnapping", "Lansingburgh Weekly Chronicle", August 8, 1866

1867

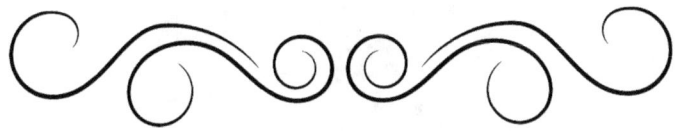

Jackson gave numerous performances on the ice in Gothenburg in January[202]. Upon his return to Stockholm, he continued giving performances on Nybroviken Bay and at the Kungliga Stora Theatern,[203] performing his skating ballet during the "Les Patineurs" scene in Giacomo Meyerbeer's opera "Le prophète".[204]

A wave of enterprising Swedish merchants used his name or likeness to sell their wares. An alcoholic drink called Skridsko Punsch (Skating Punch)[205] went on the market, as did Skridskokungen or Jackson Haines cigars, sold by the Finnilä tobacco factory.[206] These were some of the first products in history ever marketed using a specific skater's image.

---

202 "Göteborgs Handels- Och Sjöfartstidning", January 17, 1867
203 "Dagens Nyheter", February 8 and 9, 1867
204 "Dagens Nyheter", February 11, 1867
205 Advertising, "Dagens Nyheter", March 27, 1867; Correspondence with Eva Lenneman, Intendent, Spritmuseum; Correspondence with Anna Katriina Puikko, Curator of Information Service, K.H. Renlunds Museum, April 14, 2023; Records of K.H. Renlunds Museum
206 Advertising, "Öresund Posten", February 25, 1867

In February, King Carl XV of Sweden bestowed him with the royal gold medal Litteris et Artibus[207], a gold medallion depicting a crown, which he wore on his

---

207 Correspondence with Christian Thorén, Senior Curator, Chancery of the Royal Orders of Knighthood, Swedish Royal Court - Kungahuset, March 2, 2023

chest.[208] The King awarded these medals very sparingly to those who made important contributions to Swedish culture and art. Jackson was only the fourth person to receive such an honour, the third being the famous Swedish opera singer Jenny Lind.[209]

In a handwritten letter to Erik Wilhelm af Edholm, the Director of the Kungliga Stora Theatern, Jackson wrote[210]:

Stockholm February 14 1867

Court Marshal Edholm
Director Royal Theatre

Sir

I have the honor to acknowledge receipt of your distinguished favor of this morning notifying me of His Royal Majesty the King's pleasure to bestow upon me his Gold Medal with crown of the 8th size.

I cannot sufficiently express the sense of gratitude and pleasure this peculiar token of His Majesty's affiliation of my art awakens in my mind. But I beg most respectfully to assure you, that among the most endearing and pleasurable remembrances I

---

208 "Nya Dagligt Allehanda", February 19, 1867
209 Letter from Jackson Haines to Andrew J. Dupignac, President of the New York Skating Club, cited in "The Ice King", "Evening Telegram", November 13, 1871
210 "Skridskokungen Jackson Haines tackar för kunglig medalj", Stockholm City Archives

cherish of my sojourn in Europe, will be that of Sweden, its Monarch, its people, and the Royal Theater of the capital.

With the most fervent homage and gratitude towards His Royal Majesty, and every sentiment of respect for yourself

I have the honor to remain

Your most aff. & humble servt.
Jackson Haines

After his performances in Stockholm, Jackson took to the stage at the theater in Malmö[211] and on ice in Gothenburg[212] before returning to Copenhagen in March[213] for a short engagement on the ice by the Kastellet Citadel.[214]

After leaving Copenhagen, Jackson returned briefly to the Russian Empire to give a private performance for the Czar, Grand Dukes and Duchesses and Imperial Family.[215] He then travelled to Prussia, where he performed at the Stadttheater before King Wilhelm I.[216] In April, he took to the stage of the Stadttheater in Hamburg and Woltersdorff-Theater and Berliner

---

211 "Malmö Handels- Och Sjöfartstidning", February 22, 1867
212 "Göteborgsposten", March 1, 1867
213 "Halmstadsbladet", March 22, 1867
214 Advertisements, "The Berlingske Politiske og Avertissementstidende", March 19, 1867
215 "Tagesnachrichten", "Mährischer Correspondent", March 1, 1865
216 "Theatre und Kunst", "Fremden-Blatt", April 9, 1867

Hoftheater in Berlin.[217] His performances in Hamburg, in particular, drew special praise as the stage he performed on was "probably the worst, most uneven and shakiest which exists."[218]

Jackson arrived in Vienna that summer. Known far and wide as "The City of Music", the Austrian capital played host to many of the era's best composers. Under the reign of Franz Joseph I, the arts flourished. Music halls, dances and concerts were all an important part of life. Publishing houses and makers of musical instruments enjoyed lucrative success. Opera and theatre were revered.[219] Johann Strauss II was at the height of his fame, having premiered his iconic waltz "An der schönen blauen Donau" ("On The Beautiful Blue Danube") just months prior to Jackson's arrival in the city.[220] If ever there was a right time and place in the Victorian era for skating to be appreciated as an art form, Vienna in 1867 was it.[221]

Jackson gave his very first performance in Vienna on July 16 at the Carl-Theater, just five months after the

---

217 "Die Auftritte des amerikanischen 'Schlittschuhkünstlers' Jackson Haines in Deutschland", Dr. Matthias Hampe, "Pirouette" magazine, February 2019
218 "Theatre und Kunst", "Fremden-Blatt", April 9, 1867
219 "Classical Music in Nineteenth-Century Vienna, 1800–1918", Julia Teresa Friehs, "The World of the Habsburgs"
220 "Twilight of the Habsburgs: The Life and Times of Emperor Francis Joseph", Alan Palmer, 2014
221 "Influence of the Dance on Skating", Captain T.D. Richardson, "Skating World" magazine, September 1952

Wiener Eislaufverein was founded.[222] A review in the next day's newspaper read, "The skater Jackson Haines, who at the Carl-Theater yesterday gave a guest performance, is such a charming and lovely one - a worthy miracle as Vienna has not seen for years. Namely the newcomer on the ice which the guest produces is so hilarious [in its] sense of humour, and at the same time with such bravura and technique, that you can't stop laughing. We certainly don't err when we say that the rapture in which the audience yesterday sat will be of lasting effect. In the next few weeks in Vienna theater circles will only speak of Jackson Haines."[223] Another critic raved, "The star of the evening... was the skate dancer Herr Jackson Haines, whose performances are truly surprising. Mister Jackson Haines is a true virtuoso on his instrument, he handles it with mastery and great grace. His evolutions, twists, pirouettes and other tricks are truly surprising and if you follow the productions, you believe yourself deeply put into winter."[224]

Jackson became extremely popular with Viennese audiences within a matter of days,[225] and played to packed houses through the summer. In between performances, he began giving roller skating lessons to a ballerina named Leopoldine Adacker, who would later partner with him in several shows.[226]

---

[222] "150 Jahre Eiszeit: Die große Geschichte des Wiener Eislauf-Vereins", Agnes Meisinger. 2017
[223] "Theater und Kunst", "Die Debatte", July 17, 1867
[224] "Neueftes vom Theater", "Der Zwischen-Akt", July 17, 1867
[225] "Der Zwischen-Akt", July 20, 1867
[226] "Theater und Kunst", "Die Debatte", July 31, 1867

On August 25, Jackson gave his farewell performance at the Carl-Theater[227] and headed to Bratislava for an engagement at the Stadttheater. In September, he headed to Prague, where he suffered an injury to his right ankle before one of his performances at the Neustadt Theater.[228] He recovered quickly and continued on to perform in Olomouc[229] and Laibach (Ljubljana) in October.[230] He returned to Vienna in November, performing on rollers at both the Harmonie-Theater[231] and Carl-Theater.[232]

---

227 "Wiener Zeitung", August 27, 1867
228 "Prager Abendblatt", October 1, 1867
229 Advertisements, "Die Neue Zeit: Olmüzer politische Zeitung", October 11, 1867
230 Advertisements, "Vereinigte Laibacher Zeitung", October 31, 1867
231 Advertisements, "Die Debatte", November 20, 1867
232 "Theater, Kunst und Literatur", "Morgen-Post", November 29, 1867

1868

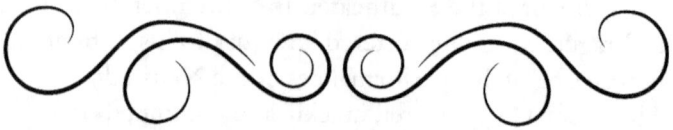

The occasion of Jackson's first performance on the ice in Vienna on January 16 was marked with great fanfare. Grandstands and a court box were erected by the Wiener Eislaufverein's rink next to the Market Hall, and a lavish buffet was prepared.[233] The "Fremden-Blatt" published this account of Haines' debut in the City of Music: "The American skater, Mr. Jackson Haines, known for his performances at the Carl-Theater... [gave] five performances in the open air in the most unfavourable conditions for skaters, but still had the greatest successes. The skating club's members wanted to give the pleasure of these surprising productions to a large audience and had taken great care to welcome the guests. The meeting place for the ladies and gentlemen of ice sports was surrounded by grandstands, from which flags waved. Walls were clad with coats of arms and emblems were adorned. A military band played before the production's start and during the performances played music. Opposite the Market Hall was a magnificent tent... [where] guests were received in festive garb bearing the club insignia... HH Erzh. Albrecht [Duke of Teschen], Karl Ferdinand, Archdukes Rainer and Wilhelm and [Maria Christina], the daughter

---

[233] "Tagesneuigkeiten", "Fremden-Blatt", January 16, 1868

of Lord Archduke Karl Ferdinand. In addition, the entire nobility of the residence, both women and gentlemen, numerous high-ranking officers and the honoured Mayor [Andreas] Zelinka. Besides the paying audience, there was also a massive non-paying audience gathered, who saw from the slopes, the railway bridge and occupied other high points. Jackson Haines appeared in his costumes, the honors and commemorative medals bestowed on him decorating the breast and began his difficult retreats on the ice, which were doubly difficult this time because of the water and heavy thaw. His skates at every turn cut deep furrows in the ice. But there was a surprising safety and grace with which he moved after the beat of music turned to a polka, and he trotted out, on tiptoe, and again on one foot, circling, moved backwards and forwards. With a strength of muscle and a rare certainty of movement on this smooth ground, he carried out the attitudes and dances with ease and grace, which was all the more reason to admire Haines. The most skilled skaters declared it an impossibility, only taking a few steps on the ice loosened by the thaw. The production consisted of five numbers, each featuring stirring applause. There was only one dissatisfied woman who tried to drown out the storm of applause with shrill whistling. Around 4 o'clock the successful production finished, the satisfied audience left the scene and the members of the ice skating club parted with the promise to follow this example in future."[234]

---

234 "Eine Production auf dem Eise", "Fremden-Blatt", January 17, 1868

The Archduke Karl Ferdinand was so moved by Jackson's skating that he returned to watch another of his performances at the Wiener Eislaufverein's rink nine days later.[235] Franz Calistus later recalled, "When one saw Haines for the first time -- gliding rhythmically over the shining ice basin of the Wiener Eislaufverein to the sounds of the Waltz which was later named for him -- then one felt was ice skating with great style was all about. There was a surety in his movement that never revealed the danger of skating on ice to the audience, only the beauty of varied gliding movement to the music. We had never seen anyone skate like this."[236]

Jackson came up with the idea[237] of putting on a benefit show for Vienna's poor, which the Wiener Eislaufverein helped organize. That January 28 show netted a profit of 1405 fl. 5 kr. - the equivalent of over ten thousand dollars in today's Canadian money – which was turned over by the Wiener Eislaufverein's chairman, Arthur Freiherr von Löwenthal, to Mayor Zelinka.[238]

Jackson expressed the wish that the money be used to distribute fuel to those living in poverty in all districts, to help keep them warm during the long Continental winter.[239]

---

235 "Eissport", "Die Debatte", January 26, 1868
236 "Die Kunst des Schlittschuhfaufens", Franz Calistus, 1891, translated by Hermann Löffler
237 "Neues Fremden-Blatt", January 28, 1868
238 "Neues Fremden-Blatt", January 30, 1868
239 "Eissport", "Wiener Zeitung", January 30, 1868

76

Jackson wanted to work with the Votivkirche to organize a further series of ice shows in the Stadtpark to raise more money for Vienna's poor, but his proposal was rejected by city officials, who feared the number of people the shows would attract might cause damage to the park facilities.[240]

Jackson left Vienna in February to make his first appearance at the Városligeti Műjégpálya in Budapest[241] This performance drew upwards of five thousand spectators, including members of the Hungarian aristocracy. [242] He next gave a series of performances on his parlour skates in Timişoara[243] and Lugosch[244]. Not long after Jackson visited Hungary and Romania, the Budapesti Korcsolyázó Egylet[245] and Kolozsvári Korcsolyázó Egylet[246] were formed.

On April 9, the Wiener Eislaufverein held an annual meeting to discuss that winter's skating season. It was reported that Jackson earned 2436 fl. from five performances he gave on the Club's ice that season, and

---

240 "Wiener Zeitung", February 1, 1868
241 "Pécs Lapok", February 13, 1868; "Házánk sa Külföld", February 13, 1868
242 "The Saturday Evening Post", June 6, 1868
243 "Fremden-Blatt", February 26, 1868
244 "Blätter für Musik, Theater und Kunst", March 13, 1868
245 "151 éve nyílt meg a városligeti jégpálya", Bálint Ternovácz, "Budapesti Levéltári Mozaikok", January 2021 (No. 28)
246 "The Development of Ice Skate Competition in Cluj in the Light of Contemporary Sports Reports (1900-1914)", András Killyeni, "Kaleidoscope: Journal of the History of Culture, Science and Medicine", Vol. 3, No. 4, July 2012

a letter from Mayor Zelinka acknowledging the Club's donation of 1405 fl. from Jackson's benefit for Vienna's poor was made available.

An excerpt from a letter submitted by Jackson was read aloud to those in attendance:

The Association should be a school of art and the ice rink no playground for jugglers, but a school for charm and grace.

This letter was "received with much glee".[247]

Jackson returned to Austria in June, spending some time in Graz with his sister Elizabeth[248], who made the long voyage from New York to visit him but ultimately decided to return to America because she was homesick.[249]

Jackson soon returned to the Carl-Theater stage, this time in duet performances with his protégé Leopoldine Adacker.[250]

Leopoldine practiced for a year before her first public appearance on parlour skates, working diligently to translate Czardas and Can Can dances to rollers.[251] The

---

247 "Neue Freie Presse", April 10, 1868
248 "Grazer Volksblatt", June 14, 1868
249 "The Father of Figure Skating", Winfield A. Hird, "Skating" magazine, January 1941
250 "Theatre und Kunstnachrichten", "Neue Freie Presse", August 30, 1868
251 "Die Debatte", September 2, 1868

duo's first performances in Vienna were well-received, and they went on to tour the theaters of Brno[252] and Prague[253] together in late September. In October, the pair enjoyed a twenty-day run at the Woltersdorff-Theater in Berlin, where Leopoldine scandalized audiences by wearing a ballet dress that showed her legs.[254]

---

252 "Fremden-Blatt", September 24, 1868
253 "Fremden-Blatt", September 27, 1868
254 "Die Auftritte des amerikanischen 'Schlittschuhkünstlers' Jackson Haines in Deutschland", Dr. Matthias Hampe, "Pirouette" magazine, February 2019

1869

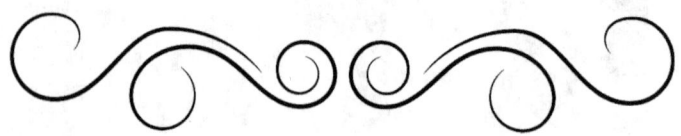

In January, Leopoldine and Jackson went on a tour of Prussia, taking to the stages of Frankfurt (Oder), Bromberg (Bydgoszcz), Danzig (Gdańsk), Elbing (Elbląg) and Königsberg (Kaliningrad)[255] before taking on a lengthy engagement at the Aarhaus-Theater in Denmark.[256]

Around this time, a rumour was circulating in Stockholm that Jackson had drowned in the Thames River.[257] The timing of this rumour suggests it may have been believed he was among the ill-fated passengers of the S.S. Princess Anne, which sunk in the Thames the previous autumn, claiming over six hundred lives.[258] Proving the rumours of his demise were very much exaggerated, Jackson arrived in Sweden in March. He

---

255 "Die Auftritte des amerikanischen 'Schlittschuhkünstlers' Jackson Haines in Deutschland", Dr. Matthias Hampe, "Pirouette" magazine, February 2019
256 Advertisements, "Kongelig privilegeret Aarhuus Stifts-Tidende", February 24, 1869
257 "Jackson Haines", "Aftonbladet", January 29, 1869
258 "Drowning in sewage: The forgotten story of the Princess Alice disaster", Stawell Heard, Royal Museums Greenwich, June 2, 2021

first gave a series of exhibitions in Malmö[259] and Gothenburg[260], where he and Leopoldine were hailed as "The Skating King and His Queen".[261] One of these exhibitions was held in conjunction with a presentation of Giuseppe Verdi's opera "Rigoletto".[262]

As in Vienna, Jackson donated proceeds of some of these performances to the poor.[263] Generosity was a recurring theme throughout his time in Europe. Some believed that he gave away much of the money he earned, leaving himself only enough for food and shelter.[264]

Leopoldine and Jackson made their way to Oslo, where Edvard Grieg had just debuted his popular "Concerto in A Minor".[265] They performed at the Theatre des Variétés in a trio[266] with a parlour skater they met in Copenhagen named Horatio Hjort, who went by the stage name

---

259 "Malmö Nya Allehanda", March 13, 1869
260 "Göteborgsposten", March 16, 1869
261 "Malmö Handels- Och Sjöfartstidning", April 20, 1869
262 Playbill for "Rigoletto" (March 21, 1869), Archives of the Musik- och teaterbiblioteket - The Music and Theater Library of Sweden
263 "Neues Fremden-Blatt", March 18, 1869
264 "Skridskostjärnan som glömdes av världen", Johan Boholm, undated article in the collection of the World Figure Skating Museum and Hall of Fame
265 "Music Library Collection Highlight: Grieg's Piano Concerto in A Minor, op. 16", Gisele Schierhorst, Stony Brok University Libraries
266 "Bergens Tidende", June 18, 1869

Horatio Syr.[267] Horatio was billed as the "Skating Prince" to Jackson and Leopoldine's "King and Queen"[268] and claimed to have once served as a sailor in The Civil War.[269]

Jackson toured Finland in July and August, performing at theaters in Helsinki[270] and Turku.[271] Neither Leopoldine nor Horatio appeared with him in these performances. By the following spring, Leopoldine was touring the Continent with a troupe of her own[272], paired with Horatio.[273]

Whether or not Jackson and Leopoldine parted on amicable terms, we do not know. It is worth noting that Jackson spent an entire year teaching Leopoldine how to skate in Vienna, only to have her team up with a skater she had known for a short time, less than a year after their first performance together.

Returning to Sweden, Jackson appeared at the Kungliga

---

267 "Kjærlighed, Sportsgribbe og Cirkusartister: Amatørførestillingar i norsk idrettsoffentlegheit 1866-1907", Gudmund Skjeldal, 2022
268 "Bergensposten", July 1, 1869
269 "Kjærlighed, Sportsgribbe og Cirkusartister: Amatørførestillingar i norsk idrettsoffentlegheit 1866-1907", Gudmund Skjeldal, 2022
270 "Helsingfors Dagblad", August 7, 1869
271 "Åbo Underrättelser", August 9, 1869
272 "Die Auftritte des amerikanischen 'Schlittschuhkünstlers' Jackson Haines in Deutschland", Dr. Matthias Hampe, "Pirouette" magazine, February 2019
273 Advertisements, "Augsburger Anzeigeblatt", May 28, 1870

Stora Theatern (Royal Opera House) in Stockholm, performing a skating scene in the operetta "Théblomma"[274], sporting his finest Victorian drag "in women's costume".[275]

In the autumn, Jackson returned to Great Britain, appearing at a benefit performance at the Standard Theatre in London[276] and six shows at the Prince of Wales Theatre in Glasgow[277] before taking up residency at the Theatre Royal in Birmingham for two months.[278] By this point in time, Jackson was being represented by Stefano Annoni de Parravicini's London theatrical agency[279], which had correspondents in Austria-Hungary, Prussia and other countries he had performed in[280].

Skating in England was progressing at a heady pace at the time of Jackson's return. In the autumn of 1869, The Skating Club flooded their natural ice rink on the grounds of the Royal Toxophilite Society. Members of the Society were able to join the Club at a reduced subscription of £2 2s if they could perform the test figures: a cross roll forwards and backwards, and a large three on each foot.[281] The first edition of Henry Eugene

---

274 Advertisements, "Nya Dagligt Allehanda", August 31, 1869
275 "Aftonbladet", August 31, 1869
276 "London Evening Standard", October 2, 1869
277 "Prince of Wales Theatre", "Glasgow Evening Citizen", November 15, 1869
278 "Public Announcements", "Birmingham Daily Gazette", December 10, 1869
279 "The London Gazette", June 13, 1876
280 Advertisements, "The Era", October 24, 1869
281 "Rules and Regulations of the Royal Toxophilite Society:

Vandervell and T. Maxwell Witham's "A System of Figure Skating" was also published. Vandervell and Witham, along with several well-heeled Londoners, were responsible for the evolution of the club's Combined Figures and the invention or popularization of several skating turns we take for granted today, including the counter, bracket and rocker. Members of The Skating Club skated in the traditional English Style, a complete juxtaposition to the artistic style Jackson performed in. The styles were as different as night and day, and while Jackson's skating was hugely popular with the general public, it wouldn't be until the Edwardian era that the style Jackson skated in – later known as the Continental or International Style – truly caught on in British figure skating circles.[282]

With an Account of the Season of 1902, List of Members, Etc.", Royal Toxophilite Society, London, 1903

282 "Our Skating Heritage", Dennis L. Bird, 1979; "Figure Skating in the Edwardian Era", Ryan Stevens, Skate Guard blog, 2020

1870

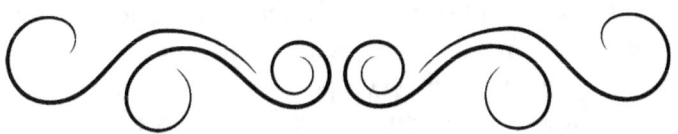

Jackson returned to Sweden in January, first giving performances on his parlour skates at the Malmö Teater[283] before heading to Stockholm, where he performed on the ice of Nybroviken Bay.[284]

In February, Jackson headed to Norway, giving exhibitions on the ice near the Vippetangen Battery[285] in Oslo during the days and performing on his parlour skates at Det Norske Teatret in the evenings.

After one of his exhibitions on the ice, a pair of local skaters named Axel Kjøl and Olaf Gjerdrum tried to upstage him. Kjøl copied Jackson's back-bend and then the duo skated a pairs act featuring several small hops and spins. It was said that the "audience received [their act] with a furious applause that probably didn't make the American especially happy." The newspapers came to Jackson's defence, stressing that his skating was high art and comparing the shtick of Axel and Olaf to "jumping over a horse and sleigh with skates on."[286] At

---

283 "Malmö Handels- Och Sjöfartstidning", January 18, 1870
284 "Hallandsposten", February 16, 1870
285 "Stavanger Amtstidende og Adresseavis", February 21, 1870
286 "Byminner: Journal of the Oslo Museum", No. 3, 1971

his final exhibition in Oslo, Jackson received a gold medal from the board of the Christiania Skøiteklub.[287] Following these performances, he performed at the Skøitesbanen in Drammens. In Drammens, he also gave exhibitions on his parlour skates at the Theatret.[288] In March, a figure skating competition was held in Oslo. Olaf Gjerdrum took first prize; Axel Kjøl was second. It didn't go unnoticed that some of the entrants were clearly trying to imitate Jackson.[289]

Jackson returned to Stockholm on March 9[290], delighting theatre-goers with his signature programs to "Lord Dundreary" and "Le prophète"[291] and debuting a very theatrical new program called "Aprez te bal masqué".[292]

From March to May, Jackson was a hit on the stages of the Teatern i Ystad[293] and Nya Teatern in Gothenburg, where his "burlesque solo dance... in a mistress's costume" was a particular draw.[294]

In May and June, Jackson was engaged at the

---

[287] "Kjærlighed, Sportsgribbe og Cirkusartister: Amatørførestillingar i norsk idrettsoffentlegheit 1866-1907", Gudmund Skjeldal, 2022; "Morgenbladet", February 11, 1870
[288] "Drammens Blad", February 26, 1870
[289] "Moss Tilskuer", February 16, 1870; "Morgenbladet", March 15, 1870; "Byminner: Journal of the Oslo Museum", No. 3, 1971
[290] "Skånska Posten", March 9, 1870
[291] "Kristianstadsbladet", March 19, 1870
[292] "Kristianstadsbladet", March 21, 1870
[293] "Ystads Tidning", April 11, 1870
[294] "Göteborgsposten", April 20, 1870

Djurgårdsteatern in Stockholm.[295] Adolf August Schéele recalled an amusing story about Jackson's off-stage antics: "Haines was a gentleman, liked by everyone who came in contact with him, and Dad Z. [C.J.L. Zetterholm] was especially delighted, because now he could refresh his talent in English. Velocipede riding had by this time become modern in Stockholm, but like many other useful things it soon degenerated into mania and decayed. Haines, who was kind of made for this kind of sport, had received from America an elegant and precious velocipede, which was carefully kept in Z's own dressing room, where Haines changed his clothing in the evenings. One evening, long before the beginning of the show, he showed his skill in riding on this peculiar means of transport. Starting behind the Hasselbacken and then continuing past the theatre, he rode standing up with his left foot in the velocipede's saddle, the right leg raised in the air and both hands on the handlebars. In this way, he came with a dizzying speed down the hill and disappeared in a cloud of dust out through the Blue Gate. The astonished onlookers thought they would never again see the man alive, but after a few moments he returned, seated properly on his wheel-legged horse. On another occasion, as a memento he presented director Z. with a precious silver vase."[296]

---

295 "Dagens Nyheter", June 10, 1870
296 "Minnen från Djurgårdsteatern 1864-1881; teaterns historia, Adolf August Schéele", 1882

After the Stockholm shows, Jackson left for The Russian Empire to teach parlour skating.[297] Enroute to St. Petersburg, he stopped briefly in Finland, but did not have time to give any performances. It was, however, reported that he also planned on visiting Moscow, Odessa and Constantinople.[298]

On October 10 and 11, Jackson appeared at the Lobe-Theater in Breslau (Wrocław), Prussia, performing several parlour skating numbers after the one-act play "Die vollkommene Frau".[299] He reappeared in Austria in November, performing during a series of plays at the

---

297 "Kristianstadsbladet", March 21, 1870; "Kristianstadsbladet", June 13, 1870
298 "Fallet Jackson Haines - Källkritiska kommentarer kring diffusionen av konståkning till Finland", Kenth Sjöblom, 1996; "Helsingfors Dagblad", July 29 and August 7 and 9, 1869
299 "Die Auftritte des amerikanischen 'Schlittschuhkünstlers' Jackson Haines in Deutschland", Dr. Matthias Hampe, "Pirouette" magazine, February 2019

Stadt-Theater in Graz[300].

Such was Jackson's popularity in Austria at the time that the ladies of Vienna sported 'Haines' hats, gloves and parasols.[301] A modern style of skate bearing Jackson's name was popular at the time. The skate consisted of a quarter of an inch steel blade, tapering to an eighth of an inch at both ends, with a rounded prow.[302] It was screwed directly into plates on the heel and toe of the boots instead of using straps. Strapless skates such as the Costello's patent model were sold in the United States as early as 1859.[303] The Jackson Haines skate was sold exclusively by the Ignaz Heiß Company in Graz for many years.[304] The model was praised by Jackson's successors for its elegance and lightness.[305]

---

300 Advertisements, "Tagespost", November 12, 1870.
301 Letter from Jackson Haines to Andrew J. Dupignac, President of the New York Skating Club, cited in "The Ice King", "Evening Telegram", November 13, 1871
302 "Figure-Skating Competitions", Edgar Syers, "The Badminton magazine of sports and pastimes", January to June 1899, Vol. VIII
303 "Additional Improvements", "The Commissioner of Patents' Journal", 1860; Advertisements, "Cleveland Daily Leader", December 1, 1860; "Improvements in Skates", "New York Daily Herald", January 13, 1861; "Central Park Skating", "Buffalo Courier", January 29, 1861; "A New Style of Skate", February 5, 1863, "The Brooklyn Daily Eagle"
304 Advertisements", "Tagespost", January 1, 1872; "Auf dem Eise: Leichtverstandliche Anleitung fur Herren, Damen und Kinder, es im Schlittschuhlaufen sehr bald zur hochsten Vollendung zu bringen", Alfred R. Seibert, 1908; "The Art of Skating", Irving Brokaw, 1910 edition
305 "Spuren auf dem Eise: Die Entwicklung des Eislaufes auf der

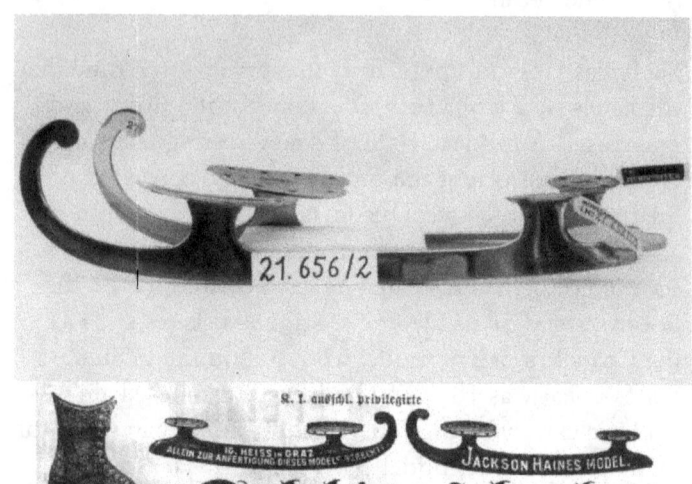

Jackson's first appearance on the ice rink of the Wiener Eislaufverein that winter took place during the afternoon on Christmas Day.[306] Accompanied by a military band[307], he proved "once again his old reputation and earned thunderous applause", attendance was not great as the temperatures were extremely cold.[308] It warmed up a bit the next day, the rink was bustling and Haines took to the ice again and was "the subject of

---

   Bahn des Wiener Eislauf-Vereins", Demeter Diamantidi, Carl
     von Korper Marienwerth, Max Wirth, 1881
306 Advertisements, "Fremden-Blatt", December 24, 1870
307 "Eissport", "Wiener Zeitung", December 27, 1870"
308 "Neue Freie Presse", December 27, 1870

admiring attention."[309]

Whether or not the glory of the stage proved solace for Jackson that year, we do not know. On July 21, on the river in Lansingburgh across from Haskell's oil cloth factory, a rowboat collided with a sailboat. Jackson's ten year-old son Abram, one of three people in the rowboat, was thrown in the water upon the impact of the collision and sank immediately to the bottom of the river. His body was found later that evening.[310] We do not know how long news of the tragedy took to reach to Jackson in Europe, but learning about the loss of his son at such a young age through a letter had to have been absolutely heartbreaking.

---

309 "Eissport", "Wiener Zeitung", December 27, 1870
310 "Hudson Daily Register", July 23, 1870

1871

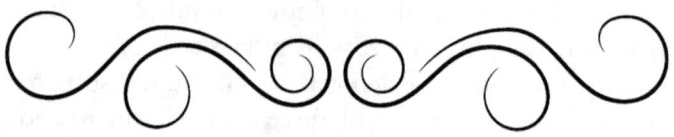

Thousands of Hungarians flocked to Jackson's first performance of 1871, held on the ice of the Városligeti Műjégpálya in Budapest on January 6. Ever the showman, Jackson started his performance by bowing to all four sides of the audience before "circling and flying to the rhythm of the music [and executing] surprising twists combined with the most appropriate 'grace', darting forward and backward and making the most amazing pirouettes on one leg, with the body bend forward, with outstretched arms like a vulture circling in the air, flying on further until his circles kept getting smaller to the dying notes of the music."[311]

The Wiener Eislaufverein celebrated the New Year with an elaborate night festival called Köstume Fest on January 11[312], organized by Carl Korper von Marienwerth.[313] Together with thirty-two of the best skaters in Vienna, who were dressed in costumes based on the paintings of Theodor Josef Ethofer[314], Jackson

---

311 "Tárcza", "Vadász- és Versenylap", January 10, 1871
312 Advertisements, "Fremden-Blatt", January 10, 1871
313 "Sportblatt: Centralblatt für die Interessen der Pferdezucht und des Sports", January 21, 1871
314 "Fremden-Blatt", January 6, 1871

stole the show. He led a procession around the giant rink illuminated by electric lights, in front of a sledge dressed in "picturesque women's garb." Jackson and the costumed skaters cheered, clapped, sang and danced on the ice until late in the evening.[315]

When Jackson gave his final performance on the ice in Vienna on January 14, there were so many in attendance that the cash registers had to be closed.[316] In frigid temperatures, with lightly falling snow, he performed a duet dressed as a bear and Savoyard with his young Viennese pupil Franz Bellazi[317] and a performance to the strains of "Les gardes de la reine" waltz.[318] Among those in attendance at this performance were Prince August of Saxe-Coburg and Gotha, Duke Alexander of Württemberg, Pauline Clémentine Marie Walburga, Princess of Metternich-Winneburg zu Beilstein, Maximilian Karl, 6th Prince of Thurn and Taxis, and Count Gyula Széchényi.[319]

When Jackson left Vienna, it was reported that he planned to return to America after his next few performances.[320] Instead, he gave a series of exhibitions at the Eisplatz of Střelecky Island in Prague in late

---

315 "Fremden-Blatt", January 12, 1871
316 "Sportblatt: Centralblatt für die Interessen der Pferdezucht und des Sports", January 21, 1871
317 "Die Presse", "January 17, 1871
318 "Eissport", "Morgen-Post", January 15, 1871
319 "Sportblatt: Centralblatt für die Interessen der Pferdezucht und des Sports", January 21, 1871
320 "Eissport", "Die Presse", January 13, 1871

January.[321] On February 2, Jackson made his debut in Warsaw, performing in subzero temperatures.[322] He appeared next in Linz, performing before a large audience at an ice rink at a riding school[323], before making his way back north towards the Russian Empire.

Jackson returned to Sweden, performing on his parlour skates at the Nya Teatern in Gothenburg in June[324] and the Djurgårdstheater in Stockholm in July and August.[325] In September, he appeared at the theater in Helsingør.[326] Grand Duke Alexei Alexandrovich of Russia, who was in Sweden for a hunt, went to watch one of Jackson's performances in Stockholm that summer.[327]

In December, Jackson surfaced in Teplice, skating on a frozen pond in the garden of the Schloss Teplice castle[328] and the Eisplatz of the Linzer Eislaufverein.

An unnamed journalist, describing one of his performances in Linz, waxed poetically about his skating: "Haines is not a skater in the ordinary sense of the word; he is a dancer on the ice, every inch an artist... We count ice skating among the arts... as Haines does,

---

321 "Prager Abendblatt", January 16, 1871; "Prager Abendblatt", January 28, 1871
322 "Vegyes", "Vadász- és Versenylap", February 10, 1871
323 "Tages-Post", February 21, 1871
324 Advertisements, "Göteborgs Handels- Och Sjöfartstidning", June 19, 1871
325 "Dagens Nyheter", July 6, 1871
326 "Dagens Nyheter", September 15, 1871
327 "Hufvudsbladet", July 18, 1871
328 Advertisements, "Teplitzer Zeitung", December 20, 1871

and whoever has seen him will surely agree with us... There is beauty found in all of his movements - power and fullness he knows how to render, just as well as grace and softness. We challenge the best ballet dancer to perform his dance with more dignified expression than Haines can... It is a pity that Meyerbeer did not live to see Haines perform his opera 'Le prophète'."[329]

In late 1871, news of the tragic Great Chicago Fire spread internationally. Jackson penned a letter to Andrew J. Dupignac, the President of the New York Skating Club, detailing his adventures in Europe and speaking of his fondness for his family. He wrote:[330]

I am the first man that has introduced skating on the boards of a royal opera house in Europe. The time will come when there will be men in my profession more capable than I am, but I am the originator. I leave a name to posterity that will remain long after I am dead and gone. To my children I leave mementos and souvenirs which I have earned in my art, and this thought has ever been my greatest reward.

Bearing in mind Jackson travelled and changed hotels constantly, and the fact it often took weeks for overseas letters to be delivered, he likely didn't know the sad truth when he penned that letter to Andrew J. Dupignac.

On the morning of July 10, his nine-year-old son

---

[329] "Tages-Post", December 31, 1871
[330] Letter from Jackson Haines to Andrew J. Dupignac, President of the New York Skating Club, cited in "The Ice King", "Evening Telegram", November 13, 1871

Eugene had walked to a dock near Holden & Defreest's Cracker Manufactory in Lansingburgh. He tied a string to a small box, dropping it in the river, playing a game the boys with him called "Make believe catch fish". After doing this several times, he lost his balance and fell into the river. The other boys called for help, but by this time he had sunk like a stone. Jackson's father and another man dove into the river several times trying to save Eugene, and finally the other man was able to bring Eugene to the surface. Every effort was made to resuscitate him, but he was unresponsive. His body was brought back to Jackson's father's home, where a local doctor unsuccessfully spent three hours trying to revive him. That afternoon, the local coroner summoned a jury for an inquest, resulting in a verdict of accidental drowning. Eugene's death was almost a year to the day that his older brother Abram had drowned in the same river.[331]

By this time, Jackson's wife Almira was living in New York and working as a dressmaker. Through "hard labour [she] not only supported herself, but was able to place herself beyond the need of want."

After the tragic deaths of Abram and Eugene, she approached Jackson's father, Alexander, appealing for restoration of custody of her daughter, Clara Louise.

Alexander refused, and the matter ended up in the Troy Courts. The same Justice who presided over the court

---

[331] "Sad Case of Drowning at Lansingburgh", "Troy Daily Times", July 11, 1871; "Lansingburgh Gazette", July 13, 1871

case involving Almira's previous alleged attempt to kidnap her sons acted as Jackson's father's counsel, but

the judge awarded custody of Clara Louise, to Almira.[332]

---

[332] "The Jackson Haines Family", "New York Clipper", September 30, 1871; "Suit For The Possession Of A Child", "Daily Albany Argus", September 19, 1871; "A Child of Jackson Haines in Court - The Mother Seeks To Recover It and Succeeds", "Troy Daily Times", September 15, 1871

PORTRAIT OF JACKSON HAINES.

1872

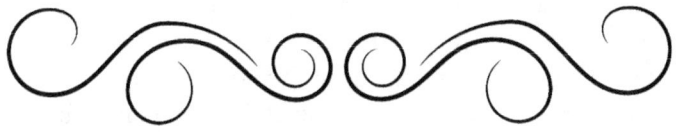

Jackson continued to perform in Graz until late January[333], when he travelled to Prague. He had arranged to give a series of exhibitions on the ice at Střelecký Island, but the temperatures dropped suddenly,. The organizers hurriedly worked to come up with an alternative. At the Neustädter Theater, which was called the Horse Market in those days, the floor seating was removed and the ground levelled and flattened. Jackson and Franz Bellazi took the ice in what was perhaps Prague's first impromptu indoor rink.[334]

Franz Bellazi remembered Jackson as an experimental skater "who performed whatever came to him at the time". He recalled, "After simultaenous entrances, Haines and I each did our program at the same time, then reunited and skated together in various forward and backward edges, a so-called Big Ubersetzer and various jumps. We then performed the Waltz together as we had in Vienna since the Haines Waltz (a solo waltz in its original form) was not suited to skating in pairs. We then

---

333 "Tagespost", January 17, 1872
334 "Prager Abendblatt", January 16, 1872; "Viennese Figure Skating", Hermann Löffler, donated to the World Figure Skating Museum and Hall of Fame on November 4, 1993

each performed a Mazurka. In the exciting second act, Haines appeared in an impressive bear costume that he had borrowed from the wardrobe of the Carl-Theatre in Vienna. I was dressed as a Savoyard who pulled the bear around on a chain and prodded him with a stick to do many clumsy antics on the ice. After a while of this, the bear grabbed the stick from me and, holding it with his paws over his shoulders, skated various slapstick-like edges to the great amusement of the audience. In the finale, he grabbed me with his paws and we skated a Waltz and exited amid great applause." Franz's father strongly objected to him touring with Jackson, so he ultimately returned to Vienna.[335]

After making his way north from Prague to St. Petersburg in early February[336], Jackson travelled to Helsinki where he performed on ice at the Brunnsparken[337] and on parlour skates at the Nya Teatern[338]. In April, he took to the stage of the Åbo Svenska Teater in Turku.[339] Jackson donated half of the proceeds from one of his Finnish shows to a local school, under the provision they use the money to buy shoes for poor children.[340]

---

335 Ibid
336 "Pietarin Sanomat", February 4, 1872
337 "Fallet Jackson Haines - Källkritiska kommentarer kring diffusionen av konstäkning till Finland", Kenth Sjöblom, 1996
338 Advertisements, "Hufvudstadsbladet", March 23, 1872
339 "Åbo Underrättelser", April 22, 1872
340 "Fallet Jackson Haines - Källkritiska kommentarer kring diffusionen av konstäkning till Finland", Kenth Sjöblom, 1996

Jackson toured Sweden in the summer, performing on his parlour skates in the communities of Sundsvall[341], Jönköping[342] and Gävle.[343] In September and October, he performed at the Mindre Teatern in Stockholm[344] and Cristinehamns Teater in Kristinehamn.[345] During his visit, King Carl XV, who had bestowed him a gold medal in appreciation of his skating,, passed away and was succeeded by his brother Oscar II.[346]

Jackson returned to the stage of the Åbo Svenska Teater in Turku in October, travelling with an acting troupe from Sweden[347] who were performing the one-act musical "Lilla Sangfageln".[348] He also gave one performance on the ice in Turku, skating on the grounds of a printer's shop, but the ice was in such poor condition that it seriously affected his performance.[349] From Finland, Jackson travelled to St. Petersburg, where he spent the Christmas holidays.[350]

Back home in America, Jackson's family's holiday season was a time of sombre reflection. Once again, there was one less chair at the dinner table - Jackson's younger

---

341 "Sundsvallposten", August 6, 1872
342 "Göteborgsposten", August 13, 1872
343 "Gefleposten", August 20, 1872
344 "Blekinge Läns Tidning", September 17, 1872
345 "Christinehamns Allehanda", October 11, 1872
346 "King Karl XV 1859-1872", De Kungliga Slotten
347 "Åbo Underrättelser", October 3, 1872
348 Advertisements, "Åbo Underrättelser", October 17, 1872
349 "Fallet Jackson Haines - Källkritiska kommentarer kring diffusionen av konstäkning till Finland", Kenth Sjöblom, 1996
350 "Arboga Tidning", January 3, 1873

sister Hannah Maria passed away that spring.[351] A short obituary in coded language in the local paper read: " The deceased died with Christian resignation, and the trials and tribulations of an unhappy life are thus ended."[352]

Though Hannah Maria was only twenty-one when she passed away, she had buried two young daughters[353] and two nephews. The fact her husband ultimately moved back to New York City, left their surviving son to be raised by Jackson's parents[354], remarried and raised his second wife's children instead[355] hints at the fact that their relationship may not have been all roses.

---

351 "Died", "The Troy Weekly Times", April 5, 1873
352 "Jottings About Town", "Lansingburgh Gazette", April 4, 1873
353 "Deaths", "New York Daily Herald", April 18, 1868; "Died", "The Troy Daily Time", April 13, 1870
354 United States Census, 1880
355 Certificate of Marriage, Etienne V. Gardiner and Sarah McKevitte, September 26, 1877

1873

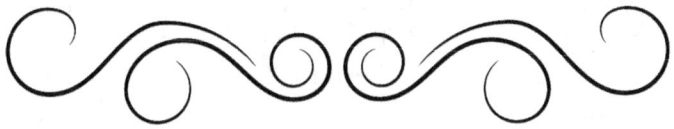

Jackson returned to Sweden in early January, performing his parlour skating act between acts of plays at the Örebro Teater[356] and the Teater in Malmö.[357]

A short tour of Norway in May and June included performances at the Theatre Bergen[358], Møllergadens Theater[359] and Theatret i Christiansfund in Oslo[360] and Teater Arendal.[361]

Jackson returned to Sweden in June, taking the stage at the Mindre Teatern in Stockholm.[362] From August to October, he was engaged at the Tivoli Gardens and Theatre in Hanover[363] and the Komödienhaus in

---

356 "Åbo Underrättelser", January 11, 1873
357 "Malmö Handels- Och Sjöfartstidning", January 29, 1873
358 "Bergens Adressecontoirs Efterretninger", June 4, 1873
359 "Kristianssands Stiftsavis og Adresse-Contors Efterretninger", May 29, 1873
360 "Christianssunds Adresseavis", June 21, 1873
361 "Vestlandska Tidende", May 29, 1873
362 "Dagens Nyheter", June 28, 1873
363 "Amusements on the Continent", "The Era", September 28, 1873; "Hannoverscher Kurier: Hannoversches Tageblatt", August 17, 1873

Münster.[364]

Jackson spent the latter part of the year in St. Petersburg[365], where he was invited to perform "at an imperial wedding.""[366] The timing of this invitation suggests this may have been the banquet following the wedding of Prince Alfred and Grand Duchess Marie Alexandrovna, held at the Winter Garden in St. Petersburg on January 23, 1874.[367]

Back in America, Jackson's family found themselves at the center of an unusual scandal involving an eccentric landlord with an interest in Spiritualism, which was extremely popular in America at the time.[368] A newspaper in Troy reported, "A highly sensational and disgraceful affair, in which the arts of old women combined with the gullibility of followers and modern Spiritualism were interestingly exhibited, took place in the village of Lansingburgh yesterday afternoon. Miss Clementina Jones owns a large frame house on the corner of River [First Avenue] and Grove [118th] streets. She, with her mother, both aged and remarkably

---

364 Programme for "Taub muß er sein! / Eine muß heiraten / Hans und Hanne / Schlittschuh-Tanz / Der Anfänger auf Schlittschuhen", October 4, 1873, Slg-Thzettel Theaterzettel Collection, Stadtarchiv Münster
365 "Åbo Underrättelser", January 26, 1874
366 "Fallet Jackson Haines - Källkritiska kommentarer kring diffusionen av konståkning till Finland", Kenth Sjöblom, 1996
367 "The Marriage of Prince Alfred and Grand Duchess Marie Alexandrovna", Royal Collection Trust
368 "That's The Spirit!", "Archives Experience" newsletter, National Archives Foundation, October 25, 2022

eccentric females, occupies the lower floors, the upper portion being rented by the Haines family, worthy and respectable people, the parents of Jackson Haines, the celebrated skater. Miss Jones considers herself a singularly persecuted female, and is constantly communicating her thousand troubles to either the police or the newspapers, who in common with others regard her as the source of all her own unhappiness, and of various annoyances and discomforts to her tenants and neighbours. Her latest idea is that her habitation is the abode of perturbed spirits... Her tenants, the Haines's, seem for some unknown reason to have found great disfavour in her eyes, and several times of late she has announced by placards on her front door that 'stolen goods were received up-stairs,' 'performances every day,' etc. On Wednesday evening a number of persons held a spiritual séance in Miss Jones's parlour, when the medium of the party discovered to the rest that silverware and bonds belonging to David Brewster, and stolen from the Waterford Bank, were secreted in Haines's apartments and in the cellar of the house, the bonds being buried in a certain designated spot in the cellar. This séance was repeated at Dr. Benton's rooms on Thursday evening. The result was that yesterday Mrs. Brewster appeared before Justice Davenport, who, upon the woman's oath that she believed and suspected upon the best of grounds that her property was in the above mentioned place, furnished her with a search warrant. In the afternoon Mr. Brewster summoned an officer and searched a certain portion of Mr. Haines's rooms. Trunks were ransacked and packages of private letters examined, but they disclosed no traces of bonds or spoons. With the aid of one of the séancers a great hole, large enough to bury the whole party, was then dug in the cellar, but the lost treasure would not turn up, although the precise spot had [been] marked off, according to the 'spirit's' directions, two feet from the wall and three feet deep. The bonds didn't appear but another officer did, who, at the insistence of Mr. Haines, arrested Mr. Brewster for malicious trespass, and proceeded with him to the station house. Mr. Brewster at once sent word to Gen. Bullard of this city, who went up and, with Wm. Bradshaw, became his bondsmen in the sum of $100 before Justice Hearmans to appear before the next criminal court in Troy. As we have said Mr. and Mrs. Haines are people of the highest respectability and honor, and the proceeding of yesterday is regarded as shamefully outrageous. The whole affair seems to have been contrived by an addled minded and maliciously inclined old woman. As to the other actors in the performance their conduct can only be regarded as silly as it was unwarrantable. Even the police declare themselves ashamed of the part they were compelled to perform in the matter."[369]

Clementina Jones may have been theatrical, but her performance certainly did not weave the same spell as Alexander and Elizabeth Haines' prodigal son, Jackson.

---

[369] "Troy Daily Times". February 8, 1873

gentlemen. Sometimes a ring would form round the great American skater, Mr. Jackson Haines, watching him execute his marvellously dexterous and graceful gyrations and gymnastics, utterly astonishing to the ordinary skater. All the while the music played, and it was near one o'clock before a crowd of skaters gathered near the pavilion gave a farewell cheer to the Royal and Imperial skaters. The entertainment of the English Skating Club was one of the most delightful evenings that heart of man, or woman either, could desire. The weather, also, which is a very great power in these parts, was on our side; the night, so black beyond the lamp-lit area, was perfectly still, and there were just the two or three degrees of frost needed to make things pleasant. A cold breeze began to blow at last from the Gulf of Finland, but that was not till 1 in the morning, when it was time for all good skaters to go home to bed.

1874

Jackson took to the ice for several performances in Vyborg in late January and early February.[370] Though he had to cancel some of his shows at the Isbanan på Salakkalahti due to illness, the ones that went off without a hitch offered a reduced price for domestic servants. This would have been an exceedingly rare opportunity for those 'below stairs' to witness world-class skating.[371]

In early February, Jackson performed at the Gymnasiasten-Schlittschuhbahn in Tallinn, Estonia,[372] before heading to St. Petersburg. On February 10, the Neva Skating Association staged a grand skating fête de nuit (night festival) on the frozen River Neva, which was attended by the Emperor and Empress of Russia, Alexander II and Maria Alexandrovna, the Prince and Princess of Wales (later King Edward VII and Queen Alexandra), Grand Duke Alexei Alexandrovich and the Crown Prince of Denmark. A report of the festivities

---

370 "Morgonbladet", January 27, 1874; "Wiborgs Tidning", January 31, 1874
371 "Fallet Jackson Haines - Källkritiska kommentarer kring diffusionen av konståkning till Finland", Kenth Sjöblom, 1996
372 "Revalsche Zeitung", February 11, 1874

recorded: "The Neva Skating Club occupies an enclosure on the River Neva, facing the English Quay, and almost opposite to the English Church. This was enlarged for the occasion, and pavilions were erected in addition to those which are usually required for the band and for the putting on of skates... For several days workmen were busily employed, and they worked during the whole of last night by the aid of electric light. The results of these efforts was visible... on the night of the fête. From the quay, a distance of about 100 yards, a boarded passage, covered with carpet, sheltered by fir trees stuck in the ice, and illuminated with coloured lanterns, led to the enclosure, at one end of which was a long covered gallery, in the centre of which was a room for ladies, and extending from it on both sides was a path of planks laid on the snow and protected on the river side by fir trees. On the right, in the centre, was a pavilion draped with red, and lighted with small chandeliers of wax candles, and behind this, half hidden by curtains was an elegant buffet, provided with refreshments both hot and cold. The device over the exterior indicated that this pavilion was intended for the Emperor, as the imperial initial in coloured lamps was conspicuous. Opposite to this was a similar pavilion, open in front and surmounted with the Prince of Wales's feathers. On each side of this were two smaller buildings, also in wood, which were occupied by military bands, and these bore the monograms A.A. and A.M. At the end, facing the ladies pavilion, was a large building, enclosed on all sides, but with three doors easily accessible by steps from the ice, and here a most liberal supply of excellent refreshments was provided during the whole of the evening to the general guests... The pavilions were painted white, and the front of each was hung with small opal lamps, relieved by festoons of red and green globes, and the buildings were connected with strings of larger lamps fastened to ornamental posts, each of which bore a small pyramid of white globes. Behind these were fir trees, planted in the ice and the dark green formed an admirable background to the scene. On each side of the extreme end was a grotto formed in blocks of ice, and in the centre of the whole a large space was enclosed by walls of ice, with projecting buttresses and an irregular battlement... Doors and windows were formed, and the latter were divided by small mullions of ice. The interior of this building was illuminated by coloured lanterns, which produced all the most exquisite colours of the most beautiful opal, and occasionally the most wonderful effects were produced by burning Bengal fire inside the ice... At 10 o'clock, by which time the general company had arrived, the scene was a splendid one, and it did not fail to elicit expressions of admiration from the royal guests in whose honour it had been devised. But little form or ceremony was needed, and the Prince and Princess of Wales, the Cesarevitch and Cesarevna, the Crown Prince of Denmark, the Grand Duke Alexis, and other members of the imperial family entered almost unnoticed, though a loud cheer greeted them as they reached the dais. Whilst they were putting on their skates, Mr. Jackson Haines, the noted American skater, performed some extraordinary feats. Soon all who were present were mingled, and princes, aristocrats, and commoners entered into the full enjoyment of the beautiful evening and the novelty of the scene. Two military bands played uninterruptedly... The dazzling glitter and indescribable colours seen through the huge blocks of ice; the gracefully gliding forms threading their way, apparently without effort; the constantly changing surface of the silver mirror, as skaters and their shadows rapidly passed across it, produced illusions which revived all the dreams of youth - and indeed, surpassed them."[373]

From the grandeur of the St. Petersburg skating fête to the grease paint of the stage, Jackson returned to Finland in March to perform on parlour skates at the Nya Teatern in Helsinki.[374] He also gave two performances before large crowds on the ice at Kaisaniemi Park.[375] In April and May, Jackson took to the stage at the Kasino-Theater in Copenhagen, Denmark.[376] That summer, while enroute to St. Petersburg, he was engaged at the Tivoli-Theater in Tallinn.[377]

While Jackson was performing in Copenhagen, American fancy skating stars Erastus Timothy 'E.T.' Goodrich and Callie Curtis were making their way to Europe. The Chicago skaters' stories were eerily similar

---

373 "A Skating Fete in Russia", from "The Home News", republished in "The Australasian", April 11, 1874
374 "Helsingfors Dagblad", January 7, 1874
375 "Helsingfors Dagblad", March 15, 1874; "Hufvudstadbladet", March 15, 1874
376 Advertisements, "Fyens Stiftstidende", April 22, 1874; Advertisements, "Dagbladet", May 30, 1874
377 "Revalsche Zeitung", August 10, 1874

to Jackson's. Both had made a name for themselves on the ice and toured America performing on parlour skates in Vaudeville-style minstrel shows. Like Jackson, Callie performed in drag on the ice. Before winning the Championships of America in Rochester in 1869[378], he had disguised himself in a veil and wig as 'Miss Godbout, the Lady from New Brunswick' in a bid to win a women's fancy competition in Buffalo.[379]

E.T. had previously toured Europe twice, performing as a double act with Alfred Moe as 'The Champion Skaters' in England, Scandinavia and Russia.[380] In their first performances in England together in conjunction with a minstrel show, E.T. and Callie plagiarized the act that Jackson had made famous - "Lord Dundreary on Skates".[381] They weren't the only Americans to 'borrow' Jackson's famous act either. Bostonian William H. Fuller had performed on parlour skates in Australia as "Lord Dundreary on the Ice" in 1866, though he claimed to do so "through an idea of his own".[382]

E.T. and Callie performed that summer in a series of shows at a former equestrian theatre in Paris known as

---

378 "Callie Curtis and Frank Swift", "New York Clipper", February 18, 1871
379 "A Decided Sell", "New York Clipper", February 20, 1869
380 Interview with E.T. Goodrich, "The Sunday Leader", March 3, 1889
381 "Liverpool Journal of Commerce", May 13, 1874
382 "Around The World on Skates", "Harper's New Monthly Magazine", Volume XL, December 1869-May 1870; Legends of Australian Ice, Ross Carpenter

the Cirque des Champs-Elysées[383], while Jackson was performing in Tallinn.[384] The three American skaters crossed paths that winter in St. Petersburg. E.T. later recalled, "Curtis and I were in St. Petersburg and gave in a covered ice rink performances when [Jackson] got there too and suggested that all three of us should go to Helsingfors in Finland, where he had been before, and give a series of performances. We were significantly better than he, both as far as demonstration and actual skill were concerned, that was not subject to comparison; and he saw that and left us the next week. Curtis and I stayed another week or two more. All he could do was about: figure eight on one foot, one vine, pirouette on both feet and a jump from forward to backward with a long run in a pose-like position and lots of dancing to the music."[385]

Jackson skated in what later was termed the Continental Style of skating, while E.T. and Callie were champions in the American Style of the time[386], which focused more on carving out intricate patterns on the ice than form or pose. For this reason, it was no wonder that E.T. did not think much of Jackson's skating. The two styles were like apples and oranges.

---

[383] "La Liberté", August 17, 1874
[384] "Revalsche Zeitung", August 10, 1874
[385] Letter from E.T. Goodrich, 1911, cited in "Das Eissportbuch", Fritz Reuel, 1928
[386] "Skating", "New York Clipper", November 16, 1867; "Callie Curtis and Frank Swift", "New York Clipper", February 18, 1871

1875

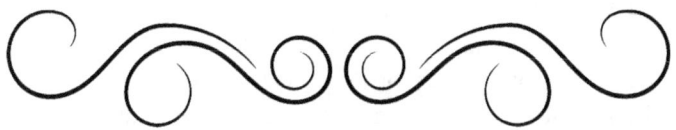

Though E.T. and Callie had no problem criticizing Jackson after the fact, they ultimately decided to follow him to Helsinki[387] and give performances at Kaisaniemi Park on February 11 and 12.[388] Jackson performed his Savoyard number, while E.T. and Callie received muted praise for a comic number "of a burlesque nature... that brought the audience into a state of shaken delight."

During one of the Helsinki shows, Jackson "was just rushing forward with the speed of the wind in his black velvet suit and the numerous circle of spectators stood in silent admiration, when suddenly the air was pierced by a roaring angry sound. Dismayed, everyone looked in the direction where the noise came from, and Jackson Haines himself was momentarily forgotten. Some curious boy or youngster had, in order to get a better view, pushed aside an old gray-haired man standing in front of him and in the process probably stepped on his toes. The old man happened to be none other than B.O.S. [the writer Berndt Otto Schauman] who, in front

---

387 "Finlands Allmänna Tidning", January 27, 1875
388 "Hufvudstadsbladet", February 10, 1875; "Åbo Underrättelser", February 13, 1875

of the whole assembled public rebuked the rude boy."[389] E.T. and Callie ultimately gave a couple more exhibitions before returning to St. Petersburg.[390] Jackson stayed in Finland.

On February 26, Jackson took to the stage in Hämeenlinna, performing on parlour skates during performances of the play "Rika Morbror".[391] In March, he travelled to Turku with a Swedish theater company, performing on his parlour skates at the Teater and then on the ice at Kupittaa Park.[392] He arrived in Pori in early April, taking to the stage of the local Teater on parlour skates and performing on the ice below a local warehouse."[393]

Jackson arrived in Vasaa in late April and gave performances on April 24 and 27, and May 2, drawing full houses at all three shows. It was announced that he was to perform in Jakobstad on May 6 and in Gamlakarleby a few days later.[394]

---

389 "Lördagens Krönika", May 14, 1921
390 "Fallet Jackson Haines - Källkritiska kommentarer kring diffusionen av konstäkning till Finland", Kenth Sjöblom, 1996
391 "Hämäläinen", February 25, 1875
392 "Åbo Underrättelser", March 9 and 19, 1875; "Sanomia Turusta", March 25, 1875
393 "Björneborgs Tidning", April 7, 10 and 14, 1875
394 "Fallet Jackson Haines - Källkritiska kommentarer kring diffusionen av konstäkning till Finland", Kenth Sjöblom, 1996

Stadt-Theater in Münster.

Donnerstag, den 1. October 1874.

Zweites Gastspiel des berühmten Schlittschuh-Tänzers
Mr. Jackson Haines.

Taub muß er sein!

Eine muß heirathen.

Hans und Hanne.

Schlittschuh-Tanz.

Der Anfänger auf Schlittschuhen.

Preise der Plätze:

Kassen-Eröffnung 6 Uhr.   Anfang 7 Uhr.

Carl Thalheim.

Jackson fell ill during the journey from Jakobstad and ended up in nearby Gamlakarleby, where he rented a room on Torikatu in the home of Klara Lindfors and her husband Wilhelm, a goldsmith.[395] One version of the story, repeated time and time again, purports that he fell ill while travelling by sled, which seems highly unlikely in May. In another version of the tale, he was sick when he was in Vasaa, but after a period of rest, walked all the way to Gamlakarleby on foot, arriving with such severe breathing difficulties that his show at the town hall had to be cancelled.[396]

After Jackson arrived in Gamlakarleby, a report in the "Vasabladet" stated, "He caught a cold and fell ill with pneumonia, which still keeps him confined to bed. A breakthrough to recovery must have already occurred, but there seems to be little hope that he will be able to perform for a long time, at least we will be denied the pleasure of seeing him on stage."[397]

Long before the days of antibiotics, doctors employed a wide variety of treatments in cases of pneumonia. These ranged from highly toxic chemicals like quicksilver and calomel (mercury chloride) to alcoholic stimulants and

---

395 Correspondence with Anna Katriina Puikko, Curator of Information Service, K.H. Renlunds Museum, April 14, 2023; Records of K.H. Renlunds Museum
396 "Skridskostjärnan som glömdes av världen", Johan Boholm, undated article in the collection of the World Figure Skating Museum and Hall of Fame
397 "Vasabladet", April 24 and May 29, 1875; "Åbo Underrättelser", June 2, 1875; "Södermanlands Läns", June 9, 1875

bloodletting, cupping and leeches. Those treating patients were also encouraged to give beef tea and milk, get plenty of sunlight and fresh air into the room and use cold-water compresses and cloths doused in turpentine. A particularly popular treatment for pneumonia at the time was a saturated tincture made from Veratrum viride - an extremely toxic plant commonly known as a corn-lily. Until the twentieth century, communities in rural Finland would have relied heavily on travelling practitioners of folk medicine, which combined herbalism with other popular methods of treatment. It is not unlikely that in Gamlakarleby, Jackson would have been treated with one or more of the methods that were popular at the time.[398]

Jackson passed away on the morning of June 23, 1875, in Gamlakarleby, during the height of Midsummer Eve celebrations.[399] An obituary, first published in Stockholm and redistributed in newspapers throughout Europe, read, "Jackson Haines attended the midsummer evening in the Finnish town of Gamla Karleby with the wish on his lips to be buried in Stockholm. Born and raised in North America, known in most European states, celebrated everywhere, he loved Sweden most of all

---

[398] "Bloodletting not necessary in the treatment of pneumonia", Dr. D.W. Young, 1870, "How to treat the sick without medicine", Dr. James C. Jackson, 1870; "Om noma", Kurt Wilhelm Envald and Knut Samuel Sirelius, 1864; "Literacy and healers's tactics in Finnish folk medicine 1850–1950", Kalle Kananoja, 2021

[399] "Björneborgs Tidning", June 23, 1875; "Nya Dagligt Allehanda", June 25, 1875; "Ölandsbladet", July 8, 1875

countries and Stockholm most of all cities. There he wished to live, there to die. Jackson Haines had well-to-do parents, who wanted to make him a well-to-do wholesaler. He was put in an office... but the ice and the skating rink drew him with marvellous power. The office stool burned his feet, which were made to walk on steel-clad shoes. Soon noticed in Boston and New York among the skating youth, he ended up outshining every member of those cities' skating clubs. Little by little he came up with the idea that skating should and could develop into a branch of the imitative art, standing on a par with dance. He developed and applied more and more this thought; and no one, who has seen him perform in advertised shows on the ice, should be able to deny that his movements in beauty, softness and grace at least rivalled the best performances of any dancer. His skating numbers - when they did not consist of comic scenes - were on; as carefully calculated, studied and practiced in advance as a ballet number. In them, Ban always described specific figures, which he himself drew in detail on the paper and for which he sought out a suitable melody, the time signatures of villages regulated the length and quantity of the steps. Consequently, he did not like to appear in public without the accompaniment of music. We have had the opportunity to see his drawings at some point, representing houses or landscapes, but usually regularly recurring curvilinear ornaments, like Valenciennes lace or rich embroidery. Only a few spectators felt that Jackson Haines went to such lengths to achieve the greatest possible beauty in movement of the men's... body, but no one will overlook that he won his goal. The 'skating king' was between 30 and 40 years old at the time of his death, which was caused by inflammation of the lungs."[400]

Jackson was only thirty-six at the time of his death.[401] He was buried at the Marian hautausmaa cemetery.[402]

---

400 "Nya Dagligt Allehanda", June 25, 1875
401 Date of death determined through his death notice "Björneborgs Tidning", June 23, 1875, which agrees with the date of death on his tombstone, coupled with the 1838 dates of birth reported in ""The Illustrated Sporting News", September 17, 1864; "Laibacher Zeitung", October 31, 1867; "Drammens Blad", January 16, 1872; "Åbo Underrättelser", November 19, 1872; "Hämäläinen", March 4, 1875. Many details published in these articles were so obscure that is a very reasonable assumption that Jackson was interviewed personally by the authors.
402 "Taitoluistelun kehittänyt Jackson Haines hurmasi Euroopan – viimeinen leposija löytyi Kokkolasta 140 vuotta sitten", Ari Vihanta, "Uutiset", September 20, 2015;

THE LEGACY

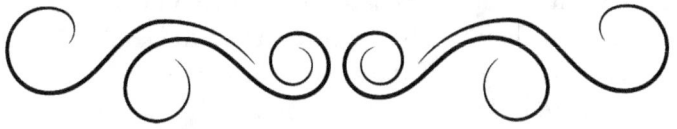

Little is known about Jackson's final days, but there have certainly been plenty of rumours.

Some have said that he was smitten a member of the theatre troupe he travelled with, and that he was helped by various local families. Long after his death, it was speculated that his cause of death was typhoid fever[403] or consumption (tuberculosis), not pneumonia.[404]

Small-town rumours have linked Jackson romantically to Klara Lindfors. When Klara passed away in 1909[405], she was buried right next to Jackson.[406] So too was her husband Wilhelm, who drowned on a sailing trip from Gamlakarleby to Kumo a year after Jackson's death.[407] Greta Wisuri took care of Klara's meals in her final

---

403 "Tanssinopettaja Jackson Haines", "Seura", February 6, 1937
404 "Jackson Haines", George Helfrich, "The Art of Skating", 1909 edition; Letter from Aatos Erkko, "Ice & Roller Skate" magazine, November 1979
405 "Dödsfall", "Österbottningen", October 26, 1909
406 Correspondence with Anna Katriina Puikko, Curator of Information Service, K.H. Renlunds Museum, April 14, 2023; Records of K.H. Renlunds Museum
407 "Suomailainen Wiralline Lehti", July 6, 1876

years,[408] and her grandmother Augusta Granlund owned the Lindfors house after their death. She recalled sleeping in the very same attic room where Jackson died. The room did not have a fireplace. The only source of heat was a chimney that came up from the kitchen.[409] There was a chest of drawers in the corner that had been there in 1875. At one point, locals trying to solve the mystery of what happened to Jackson's personal effects searched the chest of drawers for a secret compartment, but nothing was found.[410]

The fact that Klara Lindfors left a considerable sum (25,000 Finnish marks) to the Kokkola Finnish National School, with the stipulation that the interest accrued go towards scholarships for poor students is certainly worthy of mention, considering Jackson's charitable deeds and the fact we don't know with certainty what happened to his money after he passed away in the Lindfors home.[411]

---

408 "Keski-Pohjalainen", August 22, 1911
409 "Skridskokungens charm blev hans död?", "Vasabladet", March 12, 1995
410 Correspondence with Anna Katriina Puikko, Curator of Information Service, K.H. Renlunds Museum, April 14, 2023; Records of K.H. Renlunds Museum
411 "Pohjanmaalta", "Kokkola", October 30, 1909

There were also rumours linking Jackson romantically to a local accountant's daughter named Emilia Peitzius. When Jackson's parlour skates were sold at an auction years after his death, they were bought by Emilia's brother, Theodor. Theodor left them in his will to Emilia's husband, Juho Paananen. After Emilia's death, Juho donated these skates to the K.H. Renlunds Museum.[412] Theodor was also said to have purchased Jackson's ice skates. It was believed that he sold them to a talented young skater named Karl Börg, who used them until they were dull and in poor repair. A second pair was bought by a local tanner and worn for many years by his sons; a third was given to Finnish skater John Catani and given to the Swedish Skating Association and lost in a move. Well-known local sportsman and gymnastics instructor Jussi Björk claimed that Jackson's costumes were bought at auction by a theatrical family called Nyström, who used them at

---

412 Ibid

dances and masquerades for many years.[413]

Gossip about Jackson having some sort of romantic relationship with a woman in Gamlakarleby are juxtaposed with another local rumour - that didn't die of pneumonia at all... but was instead poisoned by a jealous male lover.[414] There has certainly been healthy speculation about Jackson's sexuality over the years. While there is no evidence to support that Jackson wasn't exactly heterosexual, there are certainly 'pings'. He had a style that was "florid... and unbecoming of a gentleman."[415] He danced the waltz with one of his male pupils in Vienna[416] and took him on tour with him. Donning dresses, frills and notions was not something Jackson did occasionally. Drag was actually a major component in almost all of his presentations on parlour or ice skates... evidenced through the descriptions of his performances in the hundreds of nineteenth-century sources cited in this book. This, coupled with the fact he left his wife and children behind and never returned, has led many to raise their eyebrows.[417]

---

413 Jussi Björk's notes, Familjen Björks hemarkiv / Björk family archive, The local heritage archive of Kokkola
414 "Skridskokungens charm blev hans död?", "Vasabladet", March 12, 1995
415 "Artistic Impressions: Figure Skating, Masculinity, and the Limits of Sport", Mary Louise Adams, 2011
416 "Die Presse", "January 17, 1871
417 "Gay Pioneers on Ice", Patricia Nell Warren, Outsports.com, 2004' "Why is figure skating so gay?", Liz Highleyman, "LETTERS From CAMP Rehoboth", Vol. 16, No.1, February 10, 2006

The era in which Jackson lived was a time of great religious fervour. The fact that Jackson's parents were married by a pastor who held strong Calvinist beliefs[418], which were unabashedly anti-gay at the time[419], is worth consideration.

Vivian Vreeland Mausler, the one hundred and one-year-old great, great-granddaughter of Jackson's uncle Richard, was of the belief that Jackson may have been gay and went to Europe because he would have been more accepted there at the time than in America.[420]

Joseph W. Dooley, another surviving relative who has studied the family's genealogy extensively, drew an interesting comparison between Jackson and another man who dressed flamboyantly and travelled abroad during the same era – Oscar Wilde.[421] Considering the persecution members of the LGBTQ+ community faced during the Victorian era, it is hardly a wonder that many took secrets to their graves.

---

418 Marriage Record of Alexander Frazee Haines and Elizabeth Terhune Earle, New Jersey, County Marriages, 1682-1956; "Romeyn - James van Campen", "The Cyclopedia of Biblical, Theological, and Ecclesiastical Literature", 1880
419 "Calvinists", "Encyclopedia of Homosexuality", Wayne R. Dynes, 2016
420 Interview with Vivian Vreeland Mausler, March 7, 2023
421 Interview with Joseph W. Dooley, March 7, 2023

Jackson's story became lore in Kokkola. It was said that bouquets of white roses were left at his grave by a mysterious visitor at regular intervals, that the minutes from the estate auction where Jackson's parlour skates were sold disappeared and that a gentleman from America visited Gamlakarleby shortly after his death.[422]

The latter rumour begs the question - what happened to

---

[422] "Skridskokungens charm blev hans död?", "Vasabladet", March 12, 1995

Jackson's wife and surviving family members? Almira and her daughter Clara Louise moved into a small hotel in Brooklyn. They worked together as dressmakers for a time.[423] Almira later remarried "under prosperous circumstances" to J.E. Nairn[424]. She returned to the Lansingburgh area in the autumn of 1882 to have the bodies of Abram and Eugene disinterred and moved to New York City.[425] Clara Louise married an ornamental painter named Savillian Bellknap Gardiner[426] in 1884, but was widowed just three years later.[427] Clara Louise passed away from pneumonia in 1888 at the age of twenty-six.[428]

Modern sources have implied that Almira disappeared and "escaped her grief"[429] but these speculations couldn't have been further from the truth. A year and a half after Clara Louise's death, Almira was diagnosed with breast

---

423 United States Census, 1880
424 "Died", "The World", May 29, 1888
425 "Lansingburgh", "Troy Daily Times". November 23, 1882; Correspondence with Cypress Hill Cemetery, December 31, 2013, from the records of the Lansingburgh Historical Society
426 Marriage Certificate of Clara Louise Haines and Savillian Bellknap Gardiner, September 15, 1884, The New York City Municipal Archives; New York State Census, 1875
427 Gravestone, Gardnertown Cemetery, Orange County, New York; "Gardnertown Cemetery Inscriptions", "The Independent Republican", October 29, 1912
428 State of New York Certificate of Death for Clara Louise Gardiner, May 27, 1888; "Died", "The World", May 29, 1888
429 "Tämä hautakivi pystytettiin USA:n taitoluistelulegendalle Kokkolaan – Jackson Hainesin ihmeellinen elämä sai lohduttoman lopun vuonna 1875", Karoliina Paananen, "Ilta-Sanomat", August 23, 2019

cancer. She endured a radical mastectomy in April of 1890. She passed away in her tenement home in Manhattan on January 27, 1891 at the age of forty-seven.[430] Her causes of death were ruled to be epithelioma, carcinoma fungi and exhaustion.[431] Though they couldn't all be together in later life, Almira and all three of her children were interred in a plot purchased by her mother in Cypress Hills Cemetery in Brooklyn.[432]

Jackson's parents remained on Peebles Island for a time, raising Hannah Maria's son John.[433] They returned to New York City in the early-to-mid 1880s, settling in Manhattan. Jackson's father Alexander worked into his early eighties[434], passing away of pneumonia complicated by asthma in 1895.[435] His mother Elizabeth died in 1901.[436]

Jackson's younger sister, Elizabeth, whom he'd skated with in his youth, worked as a telegraph operator for

---

[430] New York, New York City Municipal Deaths, 1795-1949; "Marriages and Deaths", "The New York Herald", January 28, 1891

[431] Certificate and Record and Death of Almira Bogart Nairn, January 27, 1891

[432] Correspondence from Telmo Gil, Cypress Hills Cemetery, December 21, 2013, courtesy Christopher Philippo, Lansingburgh Historical Society

[433] United States Census, 1880

[434] Trow's City Directory, 1885-1894 editions

[435] State of New York Certificate and Record of Death, Alexander F. Haines

[436] New York, New York, U.S., Extracted Death Index, 1862-1948

many years but fell on hard times later in life. She was admitted as an inmate of the New York City Home for the Aged and Infirm in Brooklyn in 1915.[437] She survived The Great War and passed away in 1919.[438] The last surviving member of Jackson's immediate family was his elder sister Sarah Augusta, who passed away in Newark in 1927.[439]

Less than three years after Jackson's passing, a pair of opportunistic parlour skaters named Jackson Grant and Arthur Collard showed up in Birmingham, England. Under false pretenses, they secured an engagement with the management at the Prince of Wales Theatre. During a run of the play "Cinderella", they were billed as Jackson Haines and Arthur C. Mayo, the Imperial Canadian Skaters.[440] The ballsy move of using the name of a deceased skating star who had performed in the same city less than a decade prior caused much confusion. Newspapers back home in America felt compelled to clarify that the man performing under the alias Jackson Haines in England in 1878 was not Jackson Haines, the great skater.[441] Fraud was fairly common in the entertainment world during the Victorian era. The identities of Scottish singer and comedian Harry Linn

---

437 New York, U.S., Census of Inmates in Almshouses and Poorhouses, 1915
438 New York, New York, U.S., Extracted Death Index, 1862-1948
439 New Jersey, Death Index, 1901-1903; 1916-1929; Obituary for Sarah Augusta Flammang
440 Correspondence with Rowan Gibbs, February 2, 2018
441 "To Correspondents", "New York Clipper", March 16, 1878

and English daredevil and swimmer Captain Matthew Webb were similarly presumed by enterprising confidence tricksters.[442]

The circumstances surrounding Jackson's final resting place were peculiar in that a proper gravestone wasn't erected at the time of his burial. A modest brass plate was all that marked his grave. In February of 1880, a Swedish theatre director named Conrad Landegren[443] organized a series of performances in Gamlakarleby, where "the so-called Kokkola couplets" written by Carl-Johan Sarén[444] were sung by a choir. Among these couplets were the following stanzas:

And Jackson Haines got his grave with us,
But keep quiet, never talk about it // A king's epitaph is on a
pine tree, But keep quiet, never talk about it.

After this performance, a correspondent for the Turku newspaper "Åbo Underrättelser" commented, "Curiously enough, no tombstone has yet been procured, although he is believed to have left behind the necessary means for such. For what reason this did not happen, no one knows except those who had to do with the matter. In any case, something should be done about the matter, because it is not appropriate that his epitaph

---

442 Correspondence with John Baxter, April 20, 2023
443 "Pohjois-Suomi", November 27, 1880
444 "Kokkola kupletter", K.H. Renlunds Museum Collections; "Skridskokungens charm blev hans död?", "Vasabladet", March 12, 1995

should be nailed to a number."[445] The stanza from the song performed in Gamlakarleby in 1880, coupled with this statement, doesn't outright imply that something untoward may have happened with any money Jackson left behind, but they cast some doubt as to the circumstances of his burial.

In 1881, a sea captain named Nylund reached out to the local freemasons, who raised a tall gray stone over Jackson's grave.[446] The inscription read:

Här hvilar
Skridskoartisten
Jackson Haines
död den 23 juni 1875
omkring 30 ä gammal.

J grafven dit du får är hvarken gerning, konst, förnuft eller vishet

Salom. Pred. 9:10

Translated to English, the first part of the inscription reads:

Here rests
The skating artist
Jackson Haines

---

445 "Korrespondens", "Åbo Underrättelser", February 24, 1880
446 "Wasa Tidning", August 30, 1881; Jussi Björk's notes, Familjen Björks hemarkiv / Björk family archive, The local heritage archive of Kokkola; Letter from Aatos Erkko, "Ice & Roller Skate" magazine, November 1979

Died June 23, 1875
About 30 years old

The biblical passage referenced is from Ecclesiastes 9:10, one translation of which is: "Whatever your hand finds to do, do it with all your might, for in the realm of the dead, where you are going, there is neither working nor planning nor knowledge nor wisdom." Some perceived this quote as a rather grim one, but decades after Jackson's death, a Kokkola journalist aptly noted that because of the strict religious views in the area at the time, this passage was likely chosen "as a warning example for those who devote themselves with too much zeal to a life of vanity."[447]

In approximately 1960, a second marker inscribed in remembrance of "the American Skating King" was installed by a Finnish chapter of Rotary International. In the 1970s, the Finnish Figure Skating Association cleaned and re-engraved the monuments at Jackson's grave. On June 23, 1975 - the one-hundredth anniversary of his death, Finnish Figure Skating Association President Aatos Erkko, Marks Evan Austad, the United States Ambassador to Finland and Vice-President of Metromedia (the parent company of Ice Capades) and other officials attended a wreath-laying ceremony at Jackson's grave.[448]

---

[447] "Amerikananen Jackson Haines, världens förste konståkare", "Österbotningen", August 29, 1948
[448] "Remembering Jackson Haines", "Skating" magazine, November 1975

Jackson's legacy to figure skating is immeasurable. Through the lessons he gave in the cities he visited, he directly contributed to the education of the next generation of skating stars. C.F. Mellin, who won the Stockholms Allmänna Skridskoklubb's competition in 1882, carefully studied every aspect of Jackson's skating.[449] Leopold Frey, a Viennese disciple, won the 1882 Internationalen Preis-Figurenlaufen (Great International Skating Tournament), one of the first international figure skating competitions of note held in Europe. Frey passed the knowledge Jackson taught him on to Gilbert Fuchs of Germany, who won the first World Championships in 1896.[450]

The Wiener Eislaufverein planned to honour Jackson in an elaborate Jubiläums-Costume-Fest slated to be held in January of 1892 to celebrate the club's twenty-fifth anniversary[451], but warm weather forced its postponement to the following winter.[452] Jackson was portrayed in "Im Reiche des Eisgottes" by Austrian skating pioneer Georg Zachariades[453], who won the bronze medal at that year's European Figure Skating Championships.[454]

---

449 "Tio vintrar på Nybroviken: Stockholms Allmänna Skridskoklubb 1884-1894", Ivar Boktryckeri, 1894
450 "Eissportbuch", Fritz Reuel, 1928
451 "Sport", "Neue Illustrirte Zeitung", December 20, 1891
452 "Der Sportsman", "Wiener Salonbatt", January 31, 1892
453 Programme of "Im Reiche des Eisgottes", January 9, 1893
454 "75 Years of European and World's Championships in Figure Skating", International Skating Union, 1967

Jackson's former students, Franz Bellazi, Demeter Diamantidi, Carl von Korper van Marienwerth and Max Wirth, also played important roles in the development of what became known as the Viennese School of skating. This Viennese or 'Continental' Style eventually became the prevailing style in America and around the world. For over a century after Jackson's death, Austrian skaters were dominant forces in international competition.[455]

In 1918, the Jackson Haines Skating Club was formed at Thomas Healy's Crystal Carnival Ice Rink at Broadway and 59th Street in New York City.[456] One of the most influential members of New York's skating community at during the post-War era was Irving Brokaw, who had made history as the first American figure skater to compete at the Olympic Games in London in 1908.[457] Through his travels abroad in Europe, Brokaw gained a great appreciation for the Continental Style of skating that Jackson had pioneered decades earlier. Irving did much to promote this style of skating in America. A.G. Spalding & Bros. manufactured a brand of skate in his name, after a pair in the style Jackson used that he had made in Sweden. He acquired a carved meerschaum cigar holder Jackson had once given as a gift and even

---

455 "Ice-Skating: A History", Nigel Brown, 1959
456 "Races at New Rink", "New York Tribune", January 10, 1918
457 "The Fourth Olympiad Being The Official Report of The Olympic Games of 1908 Celebrated in London Under the Patronage of His Most Gracious Majesty King Edward VII", International Olympic Committee, Theodore Andrea Cook, The British Olympic Council, 1909

impersonated him in the Skating Club of New York's 1923 carnival.[458] What Irving likely didn't know was that he was actually a distant relative of The Skating King. Jackson's great, great aunt Jane Earle had married John Gilbert Bogert, the adopted son of a Brokaw.[459]

Unfortunately, much of the misinformation about Jackson that has been spread over the years can perhaps be traced back to the 1909 and 1926 editions of Irving Brokaw's popular book "The Art of Skating". A German writer named George Helfrich who claimed to have been a student of Jackson's stated, among other things, that Jackson was born in Chicago and died "as a result of breaking his leg while jumping over a chair at a festival held on the Neva by Tsar Alexander II." The incorrect death years of 1870 and 1879 were also given. Irving's 1926 chapter on Jackson, based largely on stories Helfrich had told him, was conspicuously missing from the next edition of Brokaw's book.[460]

Not long after the end of World War II, another great American skating pioneer – Dick Button – went to Vienna to give an exhibition after winning the World Championships and was deeply moved by a large portrait of Jackson installed in the President's room at

---

458 "The Art of Skating", Irving Brokaw, 1926
459 "History and Genealogy of the Earles of Secaucus; With an Account of Other English and American Branches", Isaac Newton Earle, 1925; "Our Brokaw-Bragaw Heritage", Elsie E. Foster, 1967
460 "The Art of Skating", Irving Brokaw, 1926 edition; "The Art of Skating", 1928 edition

the clubhouse of the Wiener Eislaufverein.[461]

Beginning in the 1950s, the winners of the men's event at the World's and British Open Professional Ice Skating Championships were awarded a Jackson Haines Trophy.[462] Winners of this Trophy included Donald Jackson and Donald McPherson of Canada and Emmerich Danzer of Austria, who were all incidentally winners of the ISU World Championships as well.[463]

In 1976, Jackson was posthumously inducted to the World Figure Skating Hall of Fame, alongside great champions who represented countries he visited during his tour of Europe: Gillis Grafström and Ulrich Salchow of Sweden, Sonja Henie and Axel Paulsen of Norway, Karl Schäfer and Edi Scholdan of Austria and Captain T.D. Richardson and Reginald Wilkie of the United Kingdom.[464]

In late 1985, the United States Figure Skating Association hosted a magnificent ice show in Indianapolis called "Celebration... America on Ice" to mark the twenty-fifth anniversary of the Memorial Fund, which was formed in the aftermath of the fateful 1961 Sabena Crash that killed a generation of American

---

461 "Dick Button on Skates", Dick Button, 1955
462 "Editorial", "Skating World" magazine, May 1958
463 "The Almanac of Professional Figure Skating Competitions", Ryan Stevens, Skate Guard blog, May 2021
464 "A Capital Meeting", Mary L. Clarke, "Skating" magazine, June 1976

skaters, coaches and judges.[465] During a group number in the show, skaters in period garb honoured the sport's history. A flag was raised with the name Jackson Haines. A skater took center ice in a theatrical historical costume and offered an interpretation of Jackson's skating.[466] That skater was Donald Adair, who was Jackson's cousin, four times removed,[467] through the paternal line of his mother's family. Adair won the senior ice dance title at the 1986 U.S. Championships. His mother Ann Robinson was the winner of the 1943 U.S. novice women's title.[468]

The late John Mäki of Millcreek Township, Pennsylvania[469] took a keen interest in Jackson's story

---

465 "Celebration... America on Ice!", "Skating" magazine, July 1986
466 Video footage
467 Letter from John Mäki to a USFSA Official, World Figure Skating Museum and Hall of Fame, August 23, 1985; Genealogical research of the Robinson line of Jackson's family tree - Ann Robinson Adair's parents were Donald and Charlotte Robinson; her grandparents William James Robinson and Edith Wheeler; her great-grandparents Sarah Brown and Joseph B. Robinson. Ann's great-grandmother Sarah was one of Jackson's first cousins - the daughter of Jackson's uncle and aunt Sarah Haines and James S. Brown.
468 "The United States Championships", Joel B. Liberman, "Skating" magazine, April 1943; "Renée Roca and Donald Adair: Ice Dancing's Heirs Apparent", Libby Slate, "Skating" magazine, June 1985; "1986 U.S. Figure Skating Championships: A Celebration of Excellence", Lorna Simmons Holt and "Skating" staff, "Skating" magazine, March 1986
469 Obituaries, "Erie Times-News", January 12, 2012

and travelled to Kokkola (Gamlakarleby) in the 1980s. He had plans to develop a biographical screenplay about Jackson, but ultimately penned a work of historical fiction instead, of which only a limited number of copies were printed. Mäki's ultimate decision to write historical fiction instead of a biography resulted in an unusual hodge podge of rare facts interspersed with folklore, poetic license and at times, complete fiction.[470] His research notes are housed in the Collections of the World Figure Skating Museum in Colorado Springs and the New York Genealogical and Biographical Society.[471]

Aspects of John Mäki's 'investigation' into Jackson's story were very concerning. The tone of a series of letters he penned to high-ranking ISU and USFSA officials is uncomfortable to read at best. Requests read like demands. One ten-page letter contained a flowery request for American skaters to perform an exhibition in Kokkola: "The whole idea is awaken a dormant spirit,

---

[470] "Slippery Shoes: A Fairy Tale About The American Skating King", John Mäki, 1994; "Supplementary Reading To The Members Of: The Ottawa Figure Skating Club From Me", John Mäki, 1994; "Luistelijoiden kuningas jäi Suomeen", "Hämeen Sanomat", March 26, 2017; "Tämä hautakivi pystytettiin USA:n taitoluistelulegendalle Kokkolaan – Jackson Haines in ihmeellinen elämä sai lohduttoman lopun vuonna 1875", Karoliina Paananen, "Ilta-Sanomat", August 23, 2019

[471] Research notes on Jackson Haines, John Mäki, August 15, 1985, World Figure Skating Museum and Hall of Fame; "Notes on the figure skater Jackson Haines, 1840-1879?", John Mäki, "NYG&B Record", January 1989, Volume 120, Issue 1

who is buried under the tall pines in a forgotten grave, far from his native land. Here lies a task for our ice-princesses and princes who today draw circles, and perform miraculous pirouettes, all because of the genius of the master. So, may they go on this pilgrimage, with flowers, and pay tribute to the one who deserves this honor." Mäki's correspondence also had religious overtones.[472] At one point when he was in Kokkola, he took a drop of blood to Jackson's grave.[473]

In 1999, things took a further turn for the unhinged. A Finnish newspaper called "Alueviesti" published an article, with accompanying photographs that were anonymously submitted, claiming that Jackson's final resting place had been disturbed by a grave robber. That same year, the K.H. Renlunds Museum in Kokkola received a mysterious envelope that they believe may have been connected. It read, "Must not be opened until Christmas 2095" and then listed a bible quote, "Dry bones, hear the word of the Lord" (Ezekiel 37:4-10). This disturbing donation was treated as a time capsule and is stored unopened at the museum.[474]

Jackson's story was the subject of a musical play at the

---

472 Ten letters from John Mäki to USFSA and ISU Officials, World Figure Skating Museum, Colorado Springs

473 "Tämä hautakivi pystytettiin USA:n taitoluistelulegendalle Kokkolaan – Jackson Hainesin ihmeellinen elämä sai lohduttoman lopun vuonna 1875", Karoliina Paananen, "Ilta-Sanomat", August 23, 2019

474 Correspondence with Anna Katriina Puikko, Curator of Information Service, K.H. Renlunds Museum, April 14, 2023

149

Kokkola Municipal Theatre in 2005, directed by Maarit Pyökäri and written by Jukka-Pekka Rotko. The plot of "Luistelijain Kuningas" (which translates to "The King of Skaters" in English) was centered on the rumoured romance between Jackson and Emilia Peitzius, the church's disapproval of figure skating and society's lack of acceptance of Jackson's views. Juha Junttu[475], the actor who played Jackson, had no skating background. He seriously injured himself when he took the ice for the first time in the months leading up to the rehearsals for the production. After going through rehabilitation, he was able to take the stage in inline skates. He visited Jackson's grave for inspiration when preparing for the role.[476]

In advance of the run of "Luistelijain Kuningas", the management of the Kokkola Municipal Theatre reached out to a local skating club, the Juniori Hermes Taitoluistelijat, asking them to organize 'something' to generate interest in the play among the skating community. That 'something' ended up being the 1st Memorial Jackson Haines Cup. After the dissolution of the Juniori Hermes Taitoluistelijat club, the Kokkolan Taitoluistelijat revived this event. This competition is still being held today in Finland.[477]

---

[475] "Luistelijain kuningas -musikaali teatterin juhlavuoden satsaus", "Uutiset", KP24, January 18, 2005
[476] Interview with Juha Junttu, March 11, 2023; Programme, "Luistelijain Kuningas", 2005
[477] Interview with Anne Fagerström, Competition Manager, Finnish Figure Skating Association, March 22, 2023

Over the years, many have quite naturally drawn comparisonz between Jackson and other outstanding skaters who have brought innovation to the sport, particularly so those who have shown extraordinary artistic talent. What many have failed to consider is the fact that Jackson – the Father of Figure Skating – would have been absolutely crucified by the ISU judges of today, because his style was heavy on pose and more focused on interpretation than difficulty.

Over the years, skaters like Toller Cranston, Belita Jepson-Turner, Janet Lynn, John Curry, Robin Cousins, Jayne Torvill and Christopher Dean and Kurt Browning have all made particularly noteworthy contributions in the artistic development of the sport. Had it not been for Jackson's pioneering efforts – particularly his insistence that "music is just as much a necessity in skating as in dancing"[478] – the Continental or International Style in which these legendary skaters of the twentieth century performed may never have been popularized. Had he not dared to be bold and push skating in new directions, who really knows how the sport might have developed?

It is my hope that in some small way, this book has helped unravel some of the mystery surrounding the life of The Skating King.

Myths can be alluring but sometimes the truth is far more fascinating than any fairy tale.

---

478 "Washington Skating Park", "Chicago Daily Tribune", January 20, 1864

Jackson's great-grandfather Morris Earle, a patriot soldier in the American Revolutionary War

Jackson's great-grandmother Elizabeth (Terhune) Earle

FAMILY HISTORY

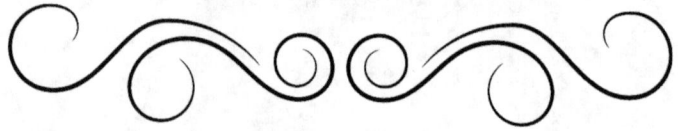

Jackson had no lineal descendants other than his children. Both of his sons, Abram and Eugene died in their youth. His daughter Clara Louise married but did not have any children. A brief summary of Jackson's family background and close relatives follows.

WIFE

Almira 'Alma' Bogart
Dress Maker
b. 1844, New York, NY
d. January 27, 1891, Manhattan, NY

CHILDREN

Abraham 'Abram' F. Haines
b. September 28, 1859, Manhattan, NY
d. July 21, 1870, Lansingburgh, NY

Eugene S. Haines
b. 1861, Manhattan, NY

d. July 10, 1871, Lansingburgh, NY

Clara Louise Haines (m. Gardiner)
Dress Maker
b. March 1862, Manhattan, NY
d. May 27, 1888, Manhattan, NY

PARENTS

Elizabeth Terhune Earle
b. January 18, 1813, Secaucus, NJ
d. November 24, 1901, Newark, NJ

Alexander Frazee Haines
Fruit Dealer, Clerk, Carpenter and Foreman
b. March 18, 1813, New York, NY
d. June 11, 1895, Manhattan, NY

SIBLINGS

Eugene Scott Morris Haines
Photographer (Haines & Wickes), Organ Builder,
Seaman and Bookkeeper
b. November 15, 1833, Hackensack, NJ
d. July 3, 1909, Brooklyn, NY

Sarah Augusta Haines (m. Flammang)
b. February 11, 1837, New York, NY
d. September 26, 1927, Newark, NJ

Hannah Maria Haines (m. Gardiner)
b. 1841, New York, NY

d. March 26, 1873, Lansingburgh, NY

Elizabeth Achsah Haines
Telegraph Operator
b. December 18, 1845, New York, NY
d. November 12, 1919, Brooklyn, NY

MATERNAL GRANDPARENTS

Maria Westervelt (m. Earle)
b. January 9, 1787, Hackensack, NJ
d. April 28, 1878, Peebles Island, NY

Morris Earle III
Sock-Maker, Hatter, Veteran of the War of 1812 (Capt. John J. Vanhorne's Company, Infantry, Col. John Dodd's Regiment, Capt.
Demorest's Company)
b. March 21, 1788, Hackensack, NJ
d. April 12, 1823, Hackensack, NJ

PATERNAL GRANDPARENTS

Hannah Frazee (m. Haines)
b. February 5, 1777, New York, NY
d. December 27, 1842, Newburgh, NY

Jackson Haines
Assessor for the Third Ward, Grocery Business Owner (Haines & Hunter)
b. July 16, 1782, New York, NY
d. April 7, 1821, Manhattan, NY

UNCLES

James S. Brown
General Store Merchant (Hardware, Books, China, Stoneware, Brandy, Gin and Spirits)
b. June 25, 1797, Monoghan, Ireland
d. February 4, 1878, Newburgh, NY

James Carlisle Ramsay
Painter
b. 1805, New York, NY
d. December 6, 1879, Newburgh, NY

William James Turnbull
Manufacturer of Window Blinds
b. March 22, 1808, New York, NY
d. October 2, 1884, Grand Rapids, MI

Eugene Scott Haines
b. January 28, 1811, Newburgh, NY
d. unknown (died without issue)

Richard Westervelt Earle
Farmer
b. October 14, 1811, Hackensack, NJ
d. August 14, 1898, Morris Plains, NJ

James Morris Earle
b. June 25, 1815, Hackensack, NJ
d. unknown (died without issue)

William Charles Clover
South American Importer, Agent (Hair Cloth Factory), Manager (Looking-Glass and Picture Frame Manufactory, Art Emporium)
b. August 14, 1817, Brooklyn, NY
d. October 19, 1909, Brooklyn, NY

Albert Terhune Earle
Cabinet Maker
b. January 1, 1819, Hackensack, NJ
d. March 8, 1883, Brooklyn, NY

AUNTS

Sarah Smith Haines (m. Brown)
b. February 22, 1805, Newburgh, NY
d. March 7, 1854, Newburgh, NY

Acshah Haines
b. May 1, 1807, Newburgh NY
d. December 22, 1828, Newburgh, NY

Isabella Oakley Haines (m. Ramsay)
b. April 24, 1809, Newburgh, NY
d. February 22, 1853, Newburgh, NY

Maria Garrison (m. Earle)
b. January 19, 1815, Paramus, NJ
d. November 19, 1873, Bogota, NJ

Sarah Earle (m. Turnbull)
b. March 22, 1817, Secaucus, NY

d. April 15, 1888, Grand Rapids, MI

Mary Earle (m. Clover)
b. March 5, 1821, Hackensack, NJ
d. January 25, 1896, Brooklyn, NY

NIECES

Aglace 'Aglee' Flammang (m. Clarkson)
b. July 14, 1857, New York, NY
d. February 1, 1906, The Bronx, NY

Sarah Flammang
b. May 5, 1860, Manhattan, NY
d. September 25, 1860, Manhattan, NY

Louise Veron Gardiner
b. May 24, 1863, NY
d. April 13, 1868, Lansingburgh, NY

Elizabeth Marie 'Lizzie' Flammang (m. Mundy)
b. July 23, 1863, New York, NY
d. December 5, 1958, Tulsa, OK

Leonie Flammang
b. December 5, 1867, Manhattan, NY
d. November 1, 1869, Newark, NJ

Mary Gardiner
b. June 26, 1868, Lansingburgh, NY
d. April 12, 1870, Lansingburgh, NY

Mary Davis Haines (m. Waldron)
b. 1868, Albany, NY
d. July 20, 1958, Amsterdam, NY

Ida Louise Flammang
b. January 1870, Newark, NJ
d. September 20, 1870, Newark, NJ

Irenne Flammang
b. February 1872, Newark, NJ
d. March 1, 1872, Newark, NJ

NEPHEWS

John Baldwin Gardiner
Manager, Photography Supplies Business, Farm Labourer
b. December 28, 1861, New York, NY
d. May 25, 1926, The Bronx, NY

John Henry Joslyn Haines
Electrician, Inventor (Vacuum Tube Lighting, Food Canning Device)
b. April 27, 1863, Lansingburgh, NY
d. June 26, 1918, Manhattan, NY

Alexander Frazee Haines II
b. October 20, 1865, NY
d. April 29, 1867, Lansingburgh, NY

Louis Pierre Flammang
Supervisor, Prudential Insurance Company

b. February 2, 1873, Newark, NJ
d. May 11, 1943, Fort Lauderdale, FL

Victor Haines Flammang
Photography and Hardware Supplies Business Owner
b. June 22, 1878, Newark, NJ
d. February 1920, Newark, NJ

BROTHERS-IN-LAW

Mathias Flammang
Superintendent, Scovill & Adams Factory, Photographer and Inventor (Photographic Camera)
b. July 1822, Grand Duchy of Luxembourg
d. April 20, 1915, Newark, NJ

Etienne Veron Gardiner
Civil War Soldier (7th Regiment, New York State Militia), Expressman, Clerk, Volunteer Firefighter and Member of the N.G.S.N.Y. (National Guard of NY State)
b. December 18, 1838, Mattituck, NY
d. February 27, 1922, Middletown, CT

SISTER-IN-LAW

Julia Frances Joslin (m. Haines)
b. June 11, 1839, Troy, NY
d. December 27, 1889, Flushing, NY

SON-IN-LAW

Savillian Bellknap Gardner

Civil War Soldier (48th Regiment, New York Infantry),
Ornamental Painter
b. December 1, 1839, Newburgh, NY
d. January 23, 1887, Newburgh, NY

FIRST COUSINS

Ann Eliza Brown (m. Carver)
b. February 18, 1827, Newburgh, NY
d. June 24, 1869, New Windsor, NY

Achsah Ann Ramsay
b. December 5, 1830, Newburgh, NY
d. September 9, 1832, Newburgh, NY

Sarah Brown (m. Robinson)
Clergyman's Wife
b. March 14, 1831, Newburgh, NY
d. January 17, 1910, Wallingford, CT

John Chichester Brown
Clerk
b. May 5, 1833, Newburgh, NY
d. February 28, 1897, New Windsor, NY

Catherine Elizabeth Earle (m. Voorhis)
b. February 13, 1835, Secaucus, NJ
d. December 5, 1913, Jersey City, NJ

Achsah Haines Brown
b. June 29, 1835, Newburgh, NY
d. March 11, 1875, Newburgh, NY

Isabella C. Ramsay
b. September 2, 1835, Newburgh, NY
d. May 7, 1845, Newburgh, NY

James Haines Ramsay
Home Decorator/Painter
b. March 8, 1838, New York, NY
d. September 12, 1921, Manhattan, NY

Lorenzo Morris Earle
b. February 4, 1839, Secaucus, NJ
d. July 8, 1840, Secaucus, NJ

Isabella Brown (m. Boyd)
b. April 18, 1839, Newburgh, NY
d. February 25, 1885, New Haven, CT

Hannah F. Ramsay
b. August 1840, Newburgh, NY
d. August 13, 1841, Newburgh, NY

Morris Franklin Earle
b. August 29, 1841, Secaucus, NJ
d. December 13, 1841, Secaucus, NJ

Morris Franklin Earle
b. April 13, 1843, Secaucus, NJ
d. August 13, 1848, Secaucus, NJ

Anna 'Annie' Richardson Clover (m. Morrison)
b. March 21, 1846, Brooklyn, NY

d. March 24, 1932, Brooklyn, NY

Henry Earle Clover
Clerk for Stock Broker, Merchant (Fur Trading and General Mercantile Store)
b. 1849, New York, NY
d. February 3, 1910, Smithtown, NY

William Charles 'Guillermo' Clover Jr.
Merchant (Fur Trading and General Mercantile Store), Clerk for Stock Broker
b. April 1, 1851, Richmond, VA
d. February 1, 1919, Laredo, TX

Margaret Eveleen Earle (m. Vreeland)
b. July 19, 1852, New York, NY
d. May 13, 1921, Adams Corner, NY

Mary Francis 'Fanny' Turnbull (m. Bryer)
Seamstress
b. September 11, 1852, Racine, WI
d. February 21, 1923, Grand Rapids, MI

Francisco Clover
Bookkeeper, Stock Broker (G. Schauman Co.), Merchant (Fur Trading and General Mercantile Store)
b. April 2, 1853, Manhattan, NY
d. February 19, 1937, Brooklyn, NY

Pauline Clover
Nurse
b. November 22, 1854, New York, NY

d. July 26, 1915, Brooklyn, NY

William James Turnbull Jr.
Wood Carver (Phoenix Furniture Company)
b. March 22, 1857, Racine, WI
d. April 20, 1918, Grand Rapids, MI

COMPETITIONS

It has long been said that Jackson won the Championships of America in 1864 and/or 1865. These accounts from local newspapers record what actually took place in those instances.

BROOKLYN, 1863

February 5, 1863, "The Brooklyn Daily Eagle"

As an item of skating intelligence, we may mention that Prof. Haines' engagement with the Union Pond has expired, and it is very doubtful whether engagement can be secured, as the Professor expects to leave the city soon, to perform elsewhere. A match was on foot between Haines and Johnson, the South Brooklyn skater, and rival of McMillan, who is also a Brooklyn man, but the arrangements were not effected.

BUFFALO, 1864

January 14, 1864, "The Buffalo Commercial"

Prospect Hill - On tomorrow afternoon, at 3 o'clock, a trial of skill is to take place between Jackson Haines and Captain Fuller, of Boston, at this popular place of resort. Some think him more adroit than Haines. The exhibitions yesterday were highly satisfactory, and all were merry as well could be. Miller's Band furnishes the music.

There was no mention of skating in any of the Buffalo newspapers on January 15, 1864.

January 16, 1864, "The Daily Courier"

Prospect Hill Skating Pond - Notwithstanding, the storm of yesterday, the ice is in good condition. Jackson Haines will appear for the last time this afternoon, and school children will be admitted for ten cents. If all is right at the Pond, flags and banners will be seen on the Niagara street cars.

DETROIT, 1864

February 2, 1864, "Detroit Free Press"

The following note explains itself:

Detroit, Feb. 1, 1864.

Mr. Jackson Haines:

Dear Sir - As you have taken upon yourself the title of champion skater, without authority or according to the rules of sporting circles, I hereby challenge you to skate with me for the championship of America, the same to take place at the Woodward Avenue Skating Park so soon as the ice is in suitable condition.

John Engler

February 6, 1864, "Detroit Free Press"

Prize skating - A skating match for a gold medal between John Engler, the champion skater, and the best skater of this city will take place this afternoon and evening at the Woodward Avenue Skating Park. Engler's reputation as a skater is good, and some beautiful skating may be expected. The pond having been lately flooded at not used, therefore a smooth surface will be had for the performance.

The only mention of skating, Jackson or John Engler in the February 7 or 8, 1864 issues of the "Detroit Free Press" is a small advertisement announcing Jackson's last appearance in Detroit.

February 9, 1864, "Detroit Free Press"

Third Street Skating Park - Yesterday afternoon and evening witnessed the most brilliant assemblage at the old skating park, to witness the final performances of the renowned Jackson Haines, that has yet favored the park with their presence. The ice was in first rate condition, and the number of skaters greatly increased, not withstanding the great centre of attention. The performance of Haines on his first appearance cast such a damper upon on operations of the city skaters, that they contented themselves with looking on in mute wonder and admiration, but like good scholars they "took notes".

APPRECIATION

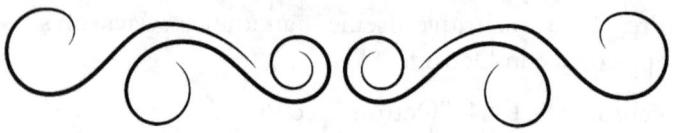

A very special thank you to the following people and organizations for their contributions to this book!

Brianne Barrett, American Antiquarian Society

John Baxter

Melanie Bazer, Information Librarian, Russell Library

Helle Brünnich Pedersen, Det Kgl. Bibliotek, The Royal Library in Copenhagen

Astra Burka, Creative Producer, Boots and Blades exhibit, Bata Shoe Museum

Yvonne Butorac

Ross Carpenter

Robin Cousins

Karen Cover, Archivist, World Figure Skating Museum and Hall of Fame

Charles F. Cummings New Jersey Information Center, Newark Public Library

Christopher Dean

Joseph W. Dooley

Jeff Doolittle, Historical Society of Newburgh

Erik Engberg, Curator of Research, K.H. Renlunds Museum, Kokkola

Bill Fitsell

Anne Fagerström, Competition Manager, Suomen Taitoluisteluliitto (Finnish Figure Skating Association)

Peggy Fleming Jenkins and Greg Jenkins

Susann Forsberg, Director of Libraries, Kokkolan kaupunginkirjasto/Karleby stadsbibliotek

Rowan Gibbs

Lena Gustafsson, Archivist, Musik- och teaterbiblioteket - The Music and Theater Library of Sweden

Lena Gyltman, Västergötlands museum

Dr. Matthias Hampe

Elaine Hooper, Historian, British Ice Skating

Aleksandra Huhtala-Labzounov

Arvid Jakobsson, Acting Palace Librarian, Keeper of the Bernadotte Archive, The Bernadotte Library, Swedish Royal Court – Kungahuset

Juha Junttu

Margaret Lavictoire

Jimmy Leiderman

Eva Lenneman, Intendent, Spritmuseum

Frazer Ormondroyd, Historian, British Ice Skating

Colin Parrish, Royal Archives, Private Secretary's Office, Windsor Castle

Christopher Philippo, Lansingburgh Historical Society

Anna Katriina Puikko, Curator of Information Service, K.H. Renlunds Museum, Kokkola

Jimmie Santee, Executive Director, Professional Skaters Association

Troy Schwindt, Editor, "Skating" magazine, U.S. Figure Skating

Janina Späth, Team Historische Bestände, Badische Landesbibliothek

John Stuart Swaim

Sarah Stevens, Spindle City Historical Society

Christian Thorén, Senior Curator, Chancery of the Royal Orders of Knighthood, Swedish Royal Court – Kungahuset

Jessica Tubis, Public Services Assistant, Beinecke Rare Book and Manuscript Library

Joseph Van Nostrand, Division of Old Records, New York State Unified Court System

Vivian Vreeland Mausler

Siân Wilks, Archivist (Cunard), Special Collections and Archives,

University of Liverpool Library

Karin Wiemann Grogan

Lena Wiorek, Stadsarkivet

Benjamin T. Wright, ISU and U.S. Figure Skating Historian ✝

Greg Young, The Bowery Boys Podcast

VISUAL MATERIAL

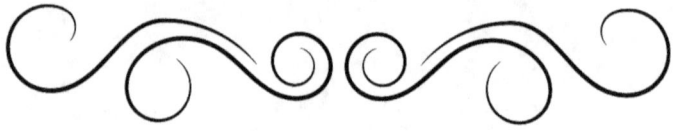

Though the majority of the visual material in this book is in the public domain, every reasonable effort has been made to trace the provenance of each photograph or illustration included.

Cover photo: Wilhelm Lundberg photograph courtesy Stadsmuseet i Stockholm, licensed under a Creative Commons International License.

1. Carte de visite by Haines & Wickes (Jackson's brother Eugene's photography business), Albany, circa July 1864. From the private collection of Jimmy Leiderman; also in the Collection of U.S. Figure Skating, "Skating" magazine. Donated by Mary Davis Haines Waldron. Picture made from an old glass negative. Used with permission.

2. Photograph courtesy Västergötlands museum. Louise Stenman photograph, donated by Walter and Lisa Rådlund, 1957. Public domain.

3. Photograph courtesy U.S. Figure Skating, "Skating

Through The Years", December 1942. Used with permission.

4. "Health Tract, No. 63: Skating" from the 1860 edition of "Hall's Journal of Health". Public domain.

5. Carte de visite from the private collection of Jimmy Leiderman. Used with permission.

6. Carte de visite from the private collection of Jimmy Leiderman. Photograph by Fd. Mulnier, Brevete S.H.D.C. 25 Boulevart des Italiens, Paris. Used with permission.

7. Engraving of the Royal Mail Steamship Africa. Photo courtesy Special Collections & Archives, University of Liverpool Library.

8. Unsigned engraving from "The Illustrated Sporting News", September 17, 1864. Public domain.

9. Engraving by Hermann Scherenberg from "Illustrirte Zeitung", February 11, 1865. Public domain (over 70 years after the death of the illustrator). Courtesy Österreichische Nationalbibliothek.

10. Illustration courtesy U.S. Figure Skating, "Skating" magazine. Cut loaned by Joel B. Lieberman. Used with permission.

64: "Mr. Jackson Haines, the Champion Skater at the Crystal Palace Dancing a Quadrille", VSCO230.00192 VSCO230, from the collection of Evert Jansen Wendell. Engraving courtesy Special Collections, Fine Arts Library, Harvard University. Used with permission; "Jackson Haines at Nybroviken, Stockholm in 1866", after a drawing by K.A. Ekvall, from "Stockholms Allmänna Skridskoklubb 1883-1923". Photo courtesy Stockholms stadsarkivet. Used with permission.

11. Photograph from "The Art of Skating" by Irving Brokaw, 1909 edition. Public domain.

12. Advertisement for Skridsko-Punsch. Photo courtesy Eva Lenneman, Intendent, Spritmuseum. Used with permission. Cigar label from the Finnilä tobacco factory. Photo courtesy K.H. Renlunds Museum. Used with permission.

13. Photograph from "The Art of Skating" by Irving Brokaw, 1909 edition. Public domain.

14. Engraving by O. Broling from "Illustreret Tidende", Volume 10, No. 489, 07/02-1869, licensed under a Creative Commons International License; Etching of Jackson Haines from Harry Stanwood's album of carte de visite photographs and newspaper etchings of entertainers. Photo courtesy General Collection, Beinecke Rare Book and Manuscript Library. Used with permission.

15. Carte de visite courtesy Musik- och teaterbiblioteket - The Music and Theater Library of Sweden. Used with permission.

16. Photograph from "International Skaters Handbook of Ice and Roller Skating", authorized by International Skating Union of America, published by Western Skating Association, Chicago, 1919. Public domain.

17. Engraving by Theodore R. Davis from "The American Velocipede", 1868, courtesy Missouri

Historical Society. No known copyright.

18. Advertisement for the Jackson Haines model of ice skates sold by the Ignaz Heiß Company from "Tagespost", January 1, 1872. Public domain. Photograph of the Jackson Haines model of skates sold by the Ignaz Heiß Company. Courtesy Wien Museum, licensed under a Creative Commons International License.

19. Photograph by Henri Osto, 1866. Courtesy Musik- och teaterbiblioteket - The Music and Theater Library of Sweden. Used with permission.

20. Photograph by Hermann Norden, courtesy Wien Museum, licensed under a Creative Commons International License.

21. Unsigned engraving from "Skating, By A Member of the London Skating Club", published the penny dreadful "Boys of the World: A Journal for Prince and Peasant", January 26, 1870. Public domain.

22. Sheet music from from the private collection of Jimmy Leiderman, printed in Budapest, 1871, found in Finland.

23. Painting from the private collection of Jimmy Leiderman. Used with permission.

24. Illustration courtesy George Grantham Bain Collection, courtesy Library of Congress. No known restrictions on publication.

25. Programme for "Taub muß er sein! / Eine muß heiraten / Hans und Hanne / Schlittschuh-Tanz / Der

Anfänger auf Schlittschuhen", October 4, 1873. Courtesy Slg-Thzettel Theaterzettel Collection, Stadtarchiv Münster. Licensed under a Creative Commons International License.

26. Engraving from "Über Land und Meer: Deutsche Illustrierte Zeitung", 16. 1866 = Jg. 8 ## No. 034, 05.1866, courtesy Bayerischeb Staatsbibliothek. Public domain; Clipping from "Western Mail", February 20, 1874. Public domain.

27. Photograph from "The Art of Skating" by Irving Brokaw, 1910 edition. Public domain

28. Photograph courtesy Det Kgl. Bibliotek, The Royal Library in Copenhagen. Used with permission.

29. Photograph by Paul Stenman of Jackson Haines' grave in Kokkola. Courtesy K.H. Renlunds Museum. Used with permission.

30. Jackson Haines' parlour skates. Photo courtesy K.H. Renlunds Museum. Used with permission.

31. Photograph from "The Art of Skating" by Irving Brokaw, 1909 edition. Public domain.

32. Portrait of Morris Earle, Jackson Haines' great-grandfather. Courtesy Joseph W. Dooley. Used with permission.

33. Portrait of Elizabeth Earle, Jackson Haines' great-grandmother. Courtesy Joseph W. Dooley. Used with permission.

34. Photograph by Aug. Jansson, Björneborg. Photo courtesy The National Museum of Finland. Used with

permission from the K.H. Renlunds Museum.

AUTHOR'S NOTE

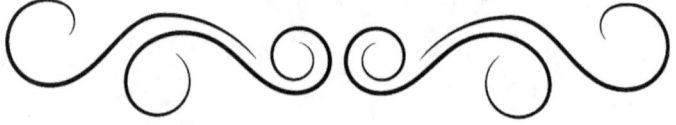

I genuinely hope that you have enjoyed reading "Jackson Haines: The Skating King" as much as I enjoyed researching and writing it.

If so, I would sincerely appreciate it if you took a few minutes to write a short review on the website of the retailer where you purchased this book, as well as popular book review sites.

Reviews are important for all books – but particularly <u>crucial</u> for those that are independently published.

Another key way you can help is by visiting your local library's website and filling out a short 'Suggest a Purchase' form.

I am grateful for your kind support in helping this important history reach the hands of more people!

OTHER BOOKS

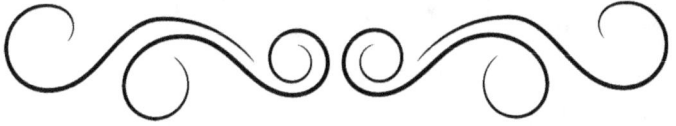

The Almanac of Canadian Figure Skating

Technical Merit: A History of Figure Skating Jumps

A Bibliography of Figure Skating

Sequins, Scandals & Salchows: Figure Skating in the 1980s

Barbara Ann Scott: Queen of the Ice-Skating

A Complete History of the World Figure Skating Championships

A Complete History of the European Figure Skating Championships

www.ingramcontent.com/pod-product-compliance
Lightning Source LLC
LaVergne TN
LVHW051558070426
835507LV00021B/2650